Ψ PB

One of the wonderful things about feng shui is that there is a remedy for just about everything.

—Richard Webster

Turn your apartment into a feng shui "home" rather than just a place to sleep at night, and watch your energy and enthusiasm soar. Whether you live in an apartment complex, a one-room studio, or a cozy dormitory, you can make subtle changes to your living area that will literally transform your life. Those who practice feng shui notice marked improvements in all areas—romance, finance, career, family, health, even in the amount of recognition they receive for their accomplishments. This latest book in Richard Webster's *Feng Shui* series concentrates on how you can increase harmonious energy in your apartment, at little or no expense.

Learn what to look for when selecting an apartment. Find out where your four positive and four negative directions are, and how to avoid pointing your bed toward the "Disaster" location. Discover the best places for other furniture, and how to remedy negative areas with plants, mirrors, crystals, and wind chimes. You'll even learn how to conduct feng shui evaluations for others. Embrace the ancient art of feng shui today and marvel at the future that unfolds.

About the Author

Richard Webster was born in New Zealand in 1946, where he still resides. He travels widely every year, lecturing and conducting workshops on psychic subjects around the world. He has written many books, mainly on psychic subjects, and also writes monthly magazine columns.

Richard is married with three children. His family is very supportive of his occupation, but his oldest son, after watching his father's career, has decided to become an accountant.

FENG SHUI

for

Apartment
Living

RICHARD
WEBSTER

2001
Llewellyn Publications
St. Paul, Minnesota 55164-0383
U.S.A.

FIRST EDITION
Third Printing, 2001

Cover design: Tom Grewe
Interior illustrations: Carla Shale and Jeannie Ferguson
Book design: Amy Rost
Editing and typesetting: Marguerite Krause
Project management: Michael Maupin

Library of Congress Cataloging-in-Publication Data
Webster, Richard, 1946–
    Feng shui for apartment living / Richard Webster. -- 1st ed.
        p. cm.
    Includes bibliographical references and index.
    ISBN 1-56718-794-3 (trade paper)
    1. Feng-shui. 2. Apartment houses--Miscellanea. I. Title.
BF1779.F4W425   1998
1343.3'337--dc21   98-28251
                                          CIP

Llewellyn Worldwide does not participate in, endorse, or have any authority or responsibility concerning private business transactions between our authors and the public.

    All mail addressed to the author is forwarded but the publisher cannot, unless specifically instructed by the author, give out an address or phone number.

Llewellyn Publications
A Division of Llewellyn Worldwide, Ltd.
P.O. Box 64383, Dept. K794-3
St. Paul, Minnesota 55164-0383
www.llewellyn.com

Printed in the United States of America

Other Books by Richard Webster

Complete Book of Palmistry (previously titled *Revealing Hands*)

Write Your Own Magic

Success Secrets

Soul Mates

Palm Reading for Beginners

Feng Shui for Success & Happiness

Feng Shui for Love & Romance

Feng Shui in the Garden

Chinese Numerology

Feng Shui for the Workplace

101 Feng Shui Tips for the Home

Astral Travel for Beginners

Spirit Guides & Angel Guardians

Aura Reading for Beginners

Seven Secrets to Success

Feng Shui for Beginners

Dowsing for Beginners

Numerology Magic

Omens, Oghams & Oracles

Dedication

For Riley G.,
psychic detective and good friend

Acknowledgments

I would like to express my grateful thanks
to T'ai Lau for his help and advice.

Contents

Introduction

Many thousands of years ago, the ancient Chinese discovered that the quality of their lives improved when they lived in harmony with the earth, rather than fighting against it. They found that life was easier if their homes faced south toward the warming sun, and were encircled by hills at their backs to protect them from the cold winds from the north. Naturally, they wanted gently flowing water in front of their homes as well.

Gradually, different ideas were tested and, over time, the basic tenets of feng shui came into being. Feng shui is approximately 5,000 years old. No one knows exactly when or how it began. It is attributed to Wu of Hsia, the first of the five mythical emperors of Chinese prehistory.

According to the story that has been handed down over the centuries, Wu was involved in irrigation work on the Yellow River when a large tortoise crawled out of the water. This was considered a good omen because, at that time, the people believed that gods lived inside the shells of turtles and tortoises. However, when they looked more closely at this tortoise, Wu and his men found that the markings on the shell created a perfect three-by-three magic square (Figure A). This was an extraordinary discovery and Wu and his wise men studied it for a long time. From this discovery came feng shui, the I Ching, Chinese astrology, and Chinese numerology. Consequently, feng shui is not a product of the "New Age." It has been around for many thousands of years.

In China, there is a saying that shows just how important feng shui is to the people. "First comes destiny, and then comes luck. Third comes feng shui, which is followed by philanthropy and education." Our destiny is revealed from our horoscope, which shows our strengths and weaknesses. Luck is harder to define, but the Chinese believe that they can improve their luck by working on the other four principles. Luck could be interpreted as a state of mind that attracts to us what we think about. Third comes feng shui, and by using it we can live in harmony with the universe. Philanthropy comes next. The ancient Chinese philosophical and religious texts emphasize that we should give selflessly, with no thought of any reward. Finally, we have education, which should be a life-long pursuit.

It is only in the last twenty-five years that people in the West have discovered feng shui. This is because people in Asian cultures considered feng shui to be so important that they deliberately concealed it. In recent years, Asian people have migrated around the world, bringing feng shui with them to their new homes. Today, you are just as likely to hear people discussing feng shui in San Francisco, Moscow,

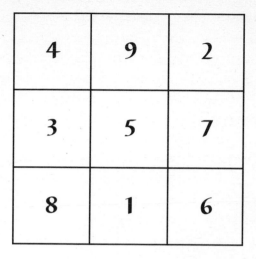

Figure A: The magic square

and Buenos Aires as you are in Hong Kong, Kuala Lumpur, or Singapore.

Today, not many people are able to live in a situation where they are facing the sun, surrounded by hills at the back of their property, with a gurgling brook in front of their home. This ideal environment remains a dream for most of us. Countless millions of people around the world live in apartment buildings. In areas where housing is in short supply, people have no choice but to accept the first apartment that becomes available. They may feel helpless and unable to do much to improve their home environment.

Fortunately, feng shui is just as useful for those who live in apartments as it is for anyone else. In fact, in many ways, it is even more useful because people in apartments frequently have special needs that have to be attended to.

By using feng shui in your apartment, you will be able to live in harmony with the earth. This will bring you increased contentment, happiness, and even abundance in every aspect of your daily life.

1

What Is Feng Shui?

Feng shui literally means "wind and water" and is the art of living in harmony with the earth. When we live in harmony with all living things, our lives progress more smoothly and we find it easier to achieve our goals. Where we live and how we arrange each room in our home can make an enormous difference to the quality of our lives.

At one time, our family lived in an apartment in a poor part of town. Because the land was low-lying, the area was covered with a dense fog every morning during the winter months. When the wind blew from a certain direction, the fog turned a dirty yellowish color and picked up an offensive smell from the sewage ponds several miles away. I was dispirited and unmotivated the entire time I lived in that neighborhood. Where I lived was having a tremendous effect on my life. When our family fortunes improved, we moved to a much better part of the city and immediately noticed that we had much more energy and enthusiasm. The negative location had sapped our energy, while the new, positive one increased it.

We are not always able to change our physical location, but we can do things inside our apartment to improve the feng shui. When we turn our apartments into "homes," rather than just somewhere to sleep at night, we are well on the way to making them positive from a feng shui point of view. This often can be achieved by changing the position of some of the furniture or increasing the light in an otherwise gloomy corner.

I am sure you have walked into an apartment and instantly felt comfortable and at home. Doubtless, you have walked into another apartment and felt vaguely uncomfortable. The first apartment was good from a feng shui point of view; the second one was not. However, with a few careful adjustments, the second apartment could become just as welcoming as the first.

By using feng shui, we are able to feel more "at home" in our apartment. When we harmonize and balance our home environment, we become happier, healthier, and more successful in every part of our lives.

We start to reap these benefits when we harness and utilize ch'i energy.

Ch'i

Ch'i is the universal life force found in all living things. It is created in many ways. Gently flowing water provides an abundant supply of ch'i energy. This is why we feel rejuvenated after spending time beside a fountain, pond, river or lake. Gentle breezes also bring ch'i to us. However, harsh gales and hurricanes carry the ch'i away, as do roaring torrents of water. When ch'i is carried away, all the good luck goes away with it.

Anything done perfectly also creates ch'i. Consequently, a skilled musician creates ch'i whenever he or she plays; a professional athlete also creates ch'i when performing at his or her best.

Nature creates ch'i all the time. Naturally beautiful surroundings, such as a magnificent mountain peak or verdant fields, create and encourage ch'i. An anonymous seventeenth century enthusiast described ch'i as being found in a place where "the hills are fair, the waters fine, the sun handsome, the breeze mild; and the sky has a new light; another world. Amid confusion, peace; amid peace, a festive air. Upon coming into its presence, one's eyes are opened; if one sits or lies, one's heart is joyful. Here ch'i gathers, and the essence collects. Light shines in the middle, and the magic goes out on all sides."[1]

Ch'i can become stale and stagnant. A pond that becomes murky or polluted creates "shar ch'i," which is negative ch'i. This also causes the good luck to vanish.

We want to encourage as much positive ch'i energy as possible to exist in our apartments, in order to increase our sense of vitality and well-being.

Yin and Yang

Ch'i can be divided into yin and yang. These are the two opposites of the universe; one cannot live without the other.

Front and back are examples of such opposites. If there was no front, there would be no back. The yin-yang symbol is a circle containing what appear to be two tadpoles. One is white with a black spot in it (yang), while the other is black with a white spot in it (yin). The spot demonstrates that wherever you find yin there will also be a small amount of yang energy, and vice versa. The yin-yang symbol is the Taoist symbol of the universe (Figure 1A).

Yin and yang are complementary, rather than opposing, elements. Yin is dark, passive, and feminine. Yang is light, active, and male. Together they create a harmonious combination.

Figure 1A: The yin/yang symbol

Yin and yang were never defined by the ancients. They preferred to come up with lists of the different opposites, and this is still a popular pastime in the East today. Here are some more examples:

Male and female

Young and old

Tall and short

Life and death

Black and white

Outside and inside

Extrovert and introvert

Father and mother

Hot and cold

Summer and winter

Heaven and earth

Night and day

Mountains and valleys

This last example is commonly discussed in feng shui. If the land is too hilly, it is said to be too yang. Land that is totally flat is said to be too yin. In feng shui we want balance. Consequently, land that is too flat can be adjusted by careful placement of rocks, statues, or a pagoda. In fact, pagodas were invented as a feng shui remedy for land that was too yin.

Yin and yang are also related to the symbolic white tiger and green dragon. The dragon is male and relates to yang energy. The tiger is female and relates to yin energy. There are two main schools of feng shui: the Form School and the

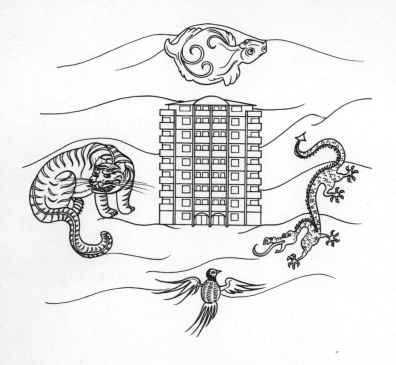

Figure 1B: The tiger and the dragon

Compass School. The Compass School uses a compass to determine suitable directions and locations. The Form School looks at the geography of the landscape, and a major concern is identifying where the dragon can be found under a hill or raised landform. A tiger is always discovered beside a dragon, and where the two symbolically couple is where the most ch'i will be found (Figure 1B).

In our apartments we also want a balance of yin and yang. If everything in our home was white, for instance, we would not feel comfortable. Imagine if everything in your bedroom was jet black. Would you feel happy sleeping there? We need a balance to create harmony.

The Five Elements

In feng shui we use the five traditional elements of Chinese astrology: fire, earth, metal, water, and wood. Everything in the world can be related to one of these five elements. In Chinese astrology you would have most or all of these elements in your chart, because your time, day, and date of birth all relate to the different elements. You can discover which element relates to your year of birth by looking in Appendix 1.

Fire

Color: Red

Direction: South

Fire is dynamic, inspiring, and understanding. It is also motivating, enthusiastic, and intelligent. Fire-element people need a great deal of variety in their lives. If your apartment building is triangular in shape or contains many sharp angles and points, you are living in a fire-shaped building.

Earth

Color: Yellow

Direction: Center

Earth is reliable, sincere, dependable, loyal, and kind. Earth enjoys handling responsibility. It is solid and stable. Earth-element people enjoy nurturing and helping others. If your apartment building is square and squat, it is considered earth-shaped.

Metal

Color: White and gold

Direction: West

Not surprisingly, metal relates to abundance and material success. It also relates to clear thinking and attention to detail. Metal-element people enjoy planning ahead and work best in an aesthetic environment. If your apartment building is rounded or curved, it is said to be metal-shaped.

Water

Color: Black and blue

Direction: North

Water relates to social activity, communication, and ultimate wisdom. It is intuitive and sensitive. Water-element people are interested in spiritual pursuits and enjoy learning. If your apartment building appears shapeless, possibly because it has been added to at different times, it is considered water-shaped.

Wood

Color: Green

Direction: East

Wood is creative, nourishing, family-minded, and flexible in approach. It relates to growth. Wood-element people enjoy challenges. If you live in a high-rise apartment building, you are living in a wood-shaped building.

The Cycles

There are two cycles, or combinations, of the five elements: the Cycle of Production and the Cycle of Destruction.

In the Cycle of Production, every element helps to produce the element that follows it in the cycle. Fire burns and creates earth. From the earth we obtain metal. Metal liquifies, which symbolizes water. Water nurtures wood. Wood burns and creates fire (see Figure 1C).

The Cycle of Destruction does the opposite. Fire burns and destroys metal. Metal destroys wood. Wood draws from and effectively weakens earth. Earth drains and weakens water. Water destroys fire (see Figure 1D).

We can incorporate these two cycles into our apartments by using elements that are most harmonious to us. For

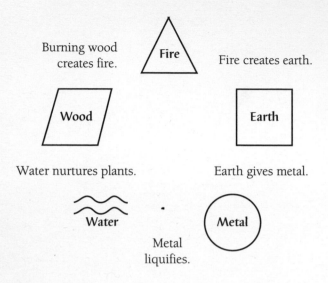

Figure 1C: The Cycle of Production

instance, if you were born in a fire year you would benefit from having potted plants or green items in your home (because wood creates fire in the Cycle of Production). However, you would not want too much water (aquariums, artificial fountains, or similar objects) or black or blue items in your apartment (because water destroys fire in the Cycle of Destruction). You would also be very happy sleeping in a bedroom on the south side of the house (because South is the direction that relates to the fire element).

Here is another example. If you were born in a metal year you would want items from the earth in your apartment (earth produces metal in the Cycle of Production).

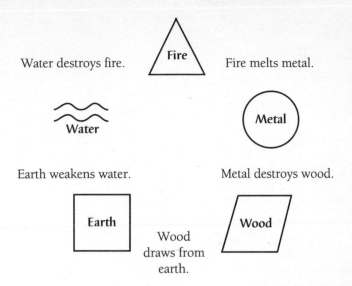

Figure 1D: The Cycle of Destruction

These could be ceramic or pottery items, or anything yellow in color. In the same way, you would want to avoid or limit the amount of red in your color scheme (fire destroys metal in the Cycle of Destruction). You would be happy sleeping in a bedroom on the west side of the house (the direction that relates to metal is west).

In general, using items that relate to your element of birth in your interior decor is beneficial. You would also be happiest living in an apartment building that relates to your element or the one preceding it in the Cycle of Production.

Naturally, if more than one person lives in the apartment, you will have to accommodate each resident's personal element. However, you may discover that you have conflicting elements. The answer to this problem is to use the elements belonging to each person in the rooms most used by that person.

There is also a Cycle of Reduction that can be used to reduce the effects of opposing energies. This cycle is the same as the Cycle of Production. If two elements are beside each other in the Cycle of Destruction they are, in effect, trying to destroy each other. We can reduce, and even eliminate, these harmful effects by finding what element is between them in the Cycle of Reduction, and using that element to balance and harmonize the situation.

For example, if the two people living in the apartment belonged to the metal and wood elements, we can see from the Cycle of Destruction that they would have problems. However, we can also see from the Cycle of Reduction that water can rectify the situation. Consequently, an aquarium or small indoor fountain would be all that was required to allow these people to live in harmony with each other.

Shars

Shars are often known as "poison arrows" and are created by straight lines and sharp angles that are directed towards you. A common example would be a path heading in a straight line directly towards the main entrance of an apartment building (Figure 1E). This forms a shar that can affect the quality of life of everyone living inside the building.

In ancient China it was believed that ghosts could travel only in straight lines. I have seen ornamental bridges in

Figure 1E: Shar aimed at a building

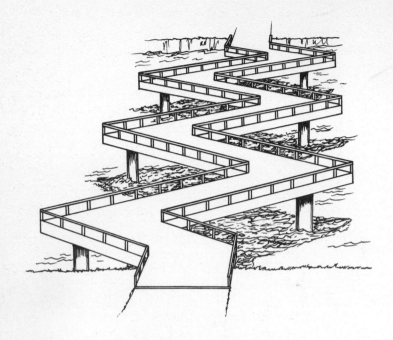

Figure 1F: Zig-zag bridge

China that zig-zag across ponds and small lakes (Figure 1F). They look very attractive and decorative, but the reason for them is feng shui rather than aesthetic. They zig-zag to prevent ghosts from crossing them.

Another common example of a shar is a sharp angle caused by the corner of a neighboring building that is oriented at a forty-five degree angle to your apartment. This sends a poison arrow to anything in its path.

Fortunately, if a shar cannot be seen, it ceases to exist. Consequently, if you are unable to see the offending corner, you do not need to worry about it. If you can see it, you can remedy the situation in a number of ways. You may simply keep the curtains drawn so that you no longer look out at it. Alternatively, you can hang up a small pa-kua mirror to reflect the shar back where it came from (Figure 1G).

Mirrors are of great importance in feng shui. Usually, they are yin, or passive, but a pa-kua mirror is yang and aggressive. This is because it is surrounded by the eight trigrams from the I Ching, which give it power and energy. A pa-kua mirror is centered on an eight-sided piece of wood. The eight-sided pa-kua has always been considered a highly auspicious shape in China.

Figure 1G: The pa-kua

Pa-kua mirrors are always small. The size is believed to concentrate their energy, but more importantly, it makes them almost invisible to the people who are sending a shar toward you.

In Hong Kong, people have mirror wars. Someone sees a shar coming toward him from a neighboring apartment and hangs up a mirror to send the shar back. The person across the road sees the mirror and puts up one of his own to reflect the mirrored image back again. Before you know it, the opponents have ten mirrors each, and finally the police are called in to end the dispute. Naturally, as soon as the police have gone the first mirror goes back up again.

Consequently, pa-kua mirrors need to be as inconspicuous as possible. They work best when hung up on the exterior wall of the building, though you can have them inside if necessary. The best position is to hang them immediately above the window or door that is affected by the shar.

You are now familiar with the basic terms that are used in feng shui. In the next chapter we will look at using feng shui when choosing your apartment building.

2

Choosing an Apartment Building

Feng shui is just as useful for apartment dwellers as it is for anyone else. In our modern world, roads can be related to rivers and buildings can represent hills and mountains.

Examine the surrounding landscape carefully when you are choosing an apartment. Ideally, the apartment building should be protected at the back, either by other apartment buildings or hills. Similar buildings on each side of the apartment building also provide support. Check carefully to ensure that they are not sending shars toward your building.

Neighboring buildings should be similar in height to the one you are considering. A neighboring building that towers over yours is considered threatening, and after a while you would find the situation increasingly oppressive. This arrangement is particularly damaging if the larger building is in front of the main entrance to your building (Figure 2A). Any large object can affect your main entrance in this way. A billboard, concrete wall, electrical transformer, even a large hill that rises directly in front of the main entrance

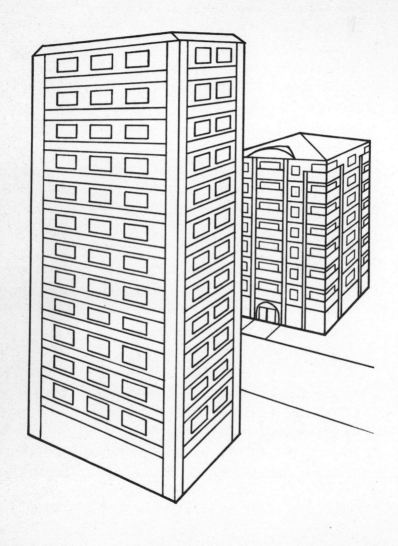

Figure 2A: Large building blocking small one

can affect the amount of ch'i that is able to accumulate in front of your apartment building.

Your apartment building should be protected in some way, either by hills or by other buildings. A building situated at the top of a hill with no protection on any side is bad from a feng shui point of view (Figure 2B). The winds blow away all the ch'i, and any water drains downhill, away from the building. You will remember that feng shui means "wind and water." We want both wind and water, but a modest amount of both. An apartment building sitting on

Figure 2B: Unprotected building

top of a hill is exposed to all the elements, and this creates "shar ch'i" (negative ch'i).

Ideally, your apartment building should be regular in shape. Square, oblong, round, and pa-kua (eight-sided) buildings are best. Irregularly shaped buildings give the impression that part of the structure is missing. For instance, an L-shaped building looks as if a piece of the building has been removed.

Ensure that the building is aesthetically pleasing. This is important, because your feelings about your home influence every area of your life. I had a friend who never invited people to her home because she considered it ugly. Consequently, she became more and more introspective and lonely. Her former vivaciousness returned as soon as she moved to an apartment in a building that she considered attractive.

Look at the color scheme of the building and ensure that it harmonizes with its environment. Certain types of buildings want to stand out and look obvious. A store that wants to be noticed by passing motorists is a good example. However, you do not want your apartment building to stick out in this way. Ideally, the color scheme should harmonize with the color that relates to your personal element. If your element is fire, you would not feel very happy living in a building that was painted blue (because water puts out fire). However, you would enjoy living in this building if your element was wood (because water nurtures wood). Similarly, a yellow building would be good for a fire person (because fire creates earth), but bad for a wood person (because wood draws from earth).

Make sure that there are no shars affecting the apartment building. The feng shui of the whole building needs to be considered before you start looking at your own apartment inside it. If your apartment building does not have a main entrance, or if you have access to your own apartment without using it, you will need to evaluate the main entrance to your apartment to ensure that no shars are affecting it.

A curving driveway leading to the main entrance is good from a feng shui point of view. This driveway should be well lit and the same width for its entire length. A straight driveway has the potential to be a shar and should be avoided.

Water in front of the main entrance is highly auspicious. This is especially the case if it is natural water. A river, lake, or harbor view is considered extremely fortunate. However, a swimming pool, pond, or fountain in front of your apartment building is also auspicious, because it creates beneficial ch'i and brings luck and good fortune to the occupants of the building. It is better for the pool to be round or oval; square or oblong pools create shars. A kidney-shaped pool should appear to envelop the building to provide protection. The pool should also be in keeping with the size of the apartment building. It is important that the water be kept clean. It is much better for the water to flow in front of the apartment building. Water passing behind the building indicates financial opportunities that cannot be utilized.

Look at the vegetation surrounding the building. Healthy-looking plants and trees indicate an abundance of beneficial ch'i. Brightly colored flowers both encourage and create ch'i, and will benefit everyone who lives in the building. An open space in front of the apartment building is extremely good, because it allows the ch'i to accumulate and benefit the residents.

The apartment building may have a parking area for the residents. It is better for such an area to be outside, rather than part of the building itself. Underground parking is also satisfactory, but ground-level parking is considered negative in feng shui. This is because the constant moving of cars creates a feeling of insecurity for the residents living above.

Next, check the lobby area. This should appear to be spacious and welcoming. The front doors can be larger than usual because apartment blocks are usually bigger than most houses. Solid doors are considered better than glass because they symbolically provide more protection.

Make sure that there are no shars heading directly toward the front doors. If the apartment building is on a T-junction, a straight road could head directly toward the entrance, creating a major shar. Shars could also come from neighboring buildings or even branches from trees that point directly toward the doors. A shar heading toward the front entrance is considered the most serious form of negative ch'i, and measures need to be taken to eliminate it.

Ensure that the apartment building has a back door. Buildings without a back door are inauspicious from a feng shui point of view (and are also potentially dangerous by any standard).

The elevators, staircases, and corridors should all be well lit and generous in size. Narrow staircases and corridors restrict the flow of ch'i; bad lighting has the same effect.

Staircases should not face the main entrance directly because this confuses the ch'i when it comes in through the front door. Ideally, the staircases should have doors that conceal them from view.

It is important that apartments on opposite sides of the hallways have doors that are aligned with each other. If the doors do not align in this way, the residents are likely to quarrel with each other.

Long hallways with a large number of doors also have the same effect. Long hallways and corridors can also create internal shars.

Examine the route you will take from the lobby to your apartment. Ideally, the staircase or elevators will be spacious and well lit. The passageways should be reasonably wide to allow the ch'i to flow freely and to enable the occupants of the building to be able to pass each other without physical contact. Look at the quality of the carpets, wall coverings, and lighting. Any defects create negative ch'i. If you rent this apartment, you will be using this route a number of times every day. Consequently, it should be bright and cheerful to encourage the ch'i and to raise your spirits.

You do not want the doors of the elevator to open directly opposite the front door to your apartment. This is because it is believed that elevators can carry your wealth away with them. You also do not want a staircase leading downward directly opposite your front door. This means that your fortunes will also be going downhill. However, a staircase heading upstairs is good, as this indicates that your fortunes are also heading upward (Figure 2C).

Finally, we need to determine if the main entrance of the apartment building is in one of your best directions. We will learn how to do this in the next chapter.

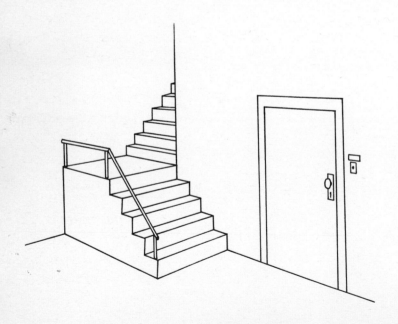

Figure 2C: An ascending stairway

3

Your Most Positive Directions

About 2,500 years ago, the Chinese invented the compass. Up until then, feng shui had been largely an art based on a study of the geography of different locations. The discovery of the compass enabled practitioners to personalize feng shui for the first time. The compass was combined with a person's personal element and his or her Chinese astrology chart to determine favorable and unfavorable directions.

Feng shui compasses are known as luo-pans. *Luo* means "reticulated" and *pan* means "dish." "Reticulated dish" is a good description of the luo-pan, which resembles a spider's web in many ways.

The luo-pan is usually square in shape. This square is divided into quarters by red thread. In the center is the compass, surrounded by a series of circles that provide information about the different directions. My luo-pan has thirteen circles of information, but I have seen some with as few as six and as many as thirty-six. The first ring contains the eight trigrams of the I Ching. The second ring contains the five elements, plus eight of the Ten Heavenly Stems from Chinese astrology. The other circles contain lucky and unlucky positions, information on determining the dates to build a house or other building, and so on. Until recently, the only feng shui compasses available were in Chinese, but it is now possible to buy English language luo-pans.[1]

The needle of the luo-pan faces south. This is because the south has always been a propitious direction for the Chinese. The cold, harsh winter winds come from the north, but the life-giving sun and warmth come from the south.

There are eight trigrams in the I Ching (Figure 3A). The original arrangement of these is the Former Heaven Sequence, which was devised by China's first emperor, Wu of Hsia. The Latter Heaven Sequence was devised in about 1143 B.C.E. by the Duke of Wen, who later founded the Chou Dynasty. The Former Heaven Sequence depicted a perfect universe. The sequence devised by the Duke of Wen shows a more practical arrangement of the trigrams that depicts a realistic view of the world we live in. Consequently, the Latter Heaven Sequence is the one that is usually used in feng shui.

The trigrams depict every possible arrangement of three broken and unbroken lines. The unbroken lines represent yang, or masculine, energy. The broken lines depict yin, or feminine, energy.

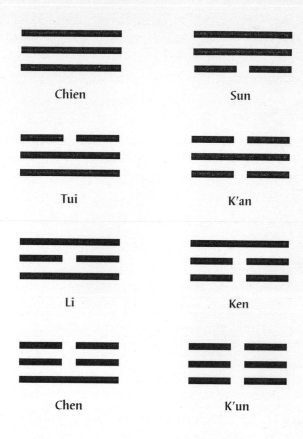

Figure 3A: The eight trigrams of the I Ching

The Individual Trigrams

Chien — The Creative

Chien is composed of three unbroken yang lines. It represents the northwest position and relates to the head of the family, usually the father. The rooms that this person would be likely to use, such as the study, den, or main bedroom are well-sited when placed in this direction. Chien is strong, persevering, and determined. The season related to Chien is late fall and early winter.

K'un — The Receptive

K'un consists of three broken yin lines. It represents the southwest and depicts the maternal qualities. K'un relates to the mother and the rooms that she would traditionally occupy, such as the kitchen, laundry, and sewing room. K'un symbolizes the relationship between husband and wife and represents summer.

Chen — The Arousing

Chen is composed of two broken yin lines above an unbroken yang line. It represents the east direction and the eldest son. Consequently, his bedroom should be on the east side of the house. Chen represents early spring and is related to decisiveness and the unexpected.

Sun — The Gentle

Sun consists of one broken yin line below two unbroken yang lines. It represents the southeast position and the eldest daughter. Consequently, her bedroom should be in this part of the house. Sun represents late spring and relates to wholesomeness, the intellect, and inner strength.

K'an — The Abysmal

K'an is made up of one unbroken yang line between two broken yin lines. It is in the north position and relates to the middle son. This part of the house is the best position for his bedroom. K'an represents winter and is related to hard work and ambition.

Li — The Clinging

Li consists of a broken yin line between two unbroken yang lines. It is in the south position and relates to the middle daughter. Naturally, her bedroom should be in the south part of the house. Li represents early summer and is related to laughter, lightness, warmth, and success.

Ken — Keeping Still

Ken is made up of two broken yin lines below an unbroken yang line. It represents the northeast direction and the youngest son. This is the best position for his bedroom. Ken represents late winter and represents stability, introspection, and consolidation.

Tui — The Joyful

Tui consists of two unbroken yang lines below a broken yin line. It represents the west position and relates to the youngest daughter. Her bedroom should be in this position in the house. Tui represents autumn and is related to happiness, pleasure, and satisfaction.

Every house and apartment can be related to a single trigram. You also have a trigram determined by your year of birth. You will be happiest in an apartment that relates positively to your personal trigram.

There is a simple formula to determine which trigram represents you. The formula varies slightly according to your sex.

If you are a man, subtract the last two digits of your year of birth from 100, and then divide by nine. The answer is ignored, but the remainder determines which trigram you belong to. If there is no remainder, the person is always a Li.

Here is an example for a man born in 1954. We subtract 54 from 100, which gives us 46. Forty-six divided by 9 goes five times, with a remainder of 1. Therefore, he is a K'an person.

Here is another example, this time for a man born in 1964. Subtracting 64 from 100 gives us 36, and 36 divided by 9 goes four times, with no remainder. He is a Li person.

If you are a woman, start by subtracting four from the last two digits of your year of birth, and then divide by nine. Again, we ignore the answer, but look at the remainder to determine which trigram you belong to.

Here is an example for a woman born in 1973. We subtract 4 from 73, which gives us 69. We divide 69 by 9, and find that it goes seven times, with a 6 remainder.

Here is another example, for a woman born in 1950. We subtract 4 from 50, which gives us 46. 9 goes five times into 46, with a remainder of 1.

If the remainder is one, the person is a K'an.

If the remainder is two, the person is a K'un.

If the remainder is three, the person is a Chen.

If the remainder is four, the person is a Sun.

If the remainder is five, the person will be a K'un if male, and a Ken if female.

If the remainder is six, the person is a Chien.

If the remainder is seven, the person is a Tui.

If the remainder is eight, the person is a Ken.

If there is no remainder, the person is a Li.

For your convenience, a chart of personal trigrams for each year is in Appendix 2.

The trigram that your apartment relates to depends on which direction the back of the building is facing. In feng shui this is known as the direction in which the back sits. Consequently, a K'an house faces south, and the back sits to the north. Figures 3B and 3C show the sitting and facing directions for each trigram.

The eight trigrams are divided into two groups: The East Four Houses, containing Li, K'an, Chen, and Sun, and the West Four Houses, containing Chien, K'un, Ken, and Tui. The favorable directions for the East Four Houses are north, south, east, and southeast. The best directions for the West Four Houses are west, northwest, southwest, and northeast.

Symbol	House Name	Back Sits	Front Faces
	Li	S	N
	K'an	N	S
	Chen	E	W
	Sun	SE	NW

Figure 3B: The East Four Houses directions

The East Four Houses

Li, K'an, Chen, and Sun all belong to the elements of water, wood, and fire. This is an excellent combination as water produces wood and wood produces fire.

This also means that apartments belonging to the East Four Houses can be enhanced by using objects belonging to these elements. Consequently, aquariums, small fountains, potted plants, freshly cut flowers, and bright lights will all improve the feng shui of apartments belonging to this group.

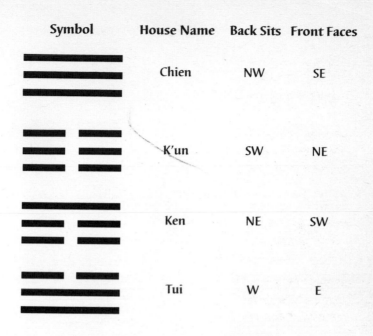

Symbol	House Name	Back Sits	Front Faces
	Chien	NW	SE
	K'un	SW	NE
	Ken	NE	SW
	Tui	W	E

Figure 3C: The West Four Houses directions

The West Four Houses

Chien, K'un, Ken, and Tui belong to the metal and earth elements. This is also a harmonious combination because metal is produced from earth. However, as the different elements do not harmonize easily, the West Four Houses clash with the East Four Houses.

The feng shui of apartments belonging to the West Four Houses improves when metallic wind chimes, metal ornaments, crystals, pottery and ceramic objects are used.

You may find it difficult to determine which trigram your apartment building belongs to if it is an irregular shape. In this instance, use a compass at the back entrance to the building to see the direction toward which it sits.

You will be happiest living in an apartment building that relates to the group you belong to. If you are a Li person, for instance, you would be happy living in an apartment building that was Li, K'an, Chen, or Sun, because these all belong to the same grouping. Naturally, the best possible arrangement is when your apartment building shares the same trigram with you. Consequently, a Chien person would be happiest living in a Chien apartment, but would also be contented living in a K'un, Ken, or Tui apartment (which all belong to the West Four Houses group).

Your apartment inside the building should also belong to the same grouping. You can determine this by using a compass at the main entrance to your apartment.

It is especially auspicious if your personal trigram, the building's trigram and your apartment's trigram all belong to the same group. An example would be if your personal trigram is Ken, the building is K'un, and the apartment is Tui. These all belong to the West Four Houses group and harmonize and support each other.

The trigrams are also used inside the apartment itself. We will cover that subject in Chapter 4.

4

Inside the Apartment

For people who live in apartments, the feng shui inside the home is more important than the feng shui outside. This is because they are frequently unable to do anything about the exterior, but do have control over what happens inside their front doors.

We want as much ch'i as possible to enter the apartment and flow easily and smoothly from room to room. Most of the ch'i comes in through the front door. Consequently, the main entrance should be well lit and appear welcoming to encourage as much ch'i as possible to come in. Ideally, you should be able to see part of the interior from the front door. The apartment should appear cheerful and spacious.

If the front door opens directly into a large room, you may wish to use a screen to cut off part of the room and create a separate, more private entrance area.

The front door should open inward. Outward-opening doors confuse and restrict the ch'i. The interior should appear spacious. The ch'i is constricted and reduced if the front door opens into a tiny lobby area, or a wall immediately in front of it. The remedy for this is to hang up a large mirror, which has the effect of symbolically doubling the size of the entrance area.

The front door also should not directly face the entrance to a toilet. Toilets create negative ch'i and should never face entrances or important rooms. If you have this situation in your apartment, keep the door to the toilet closed at all times and hang a mirror on the outside of the door to symbolically make it disappear. If you have another toilet in the bathroom, use the one facing the front door as little as possible.

Front doors should not directly face windows, because most of the ch'i that comes in the front door will go straight out the window again. A remedy for this is to use a screen to conceal the window from the front door.

Ch'i can also come in through the windows, but by far the bulk of it will come in through the front door. Your windows should be large enough to encourage ch'i in, but not so large that they affect your front door. Ideally, there should be no more than three windows to every door in the apartment. (The exception to this is the studio or single-room apartment, which may have only two doors. In this case, the ratio can be as high as 7:1.)

Stand at your front door and look for the corner that is farthest away from you, but still in view. This is your Fortu-itous Corner. Place something here that represents either your personal element, or the element that precedes yours in the Cycle of Production.

Once inside, the ch'i should be encouraged to take a meandering course through your apartment. We do not want the ch'i to move too far in a straight line, as it will flow too quickly and the beneficial effects will be lost. The worst scenario is three doors in a straight line, particularly if this includes both the front and back doors. Fortunately, there are a number of remedies for this situation. You could keep the middle door closed as much as possible. You could use a screen to hide the final doorway. You could hang a wind chime or crystal in front of the doorways to encourage the ch'i upward. Finally, you could hang two or three mirrors on each side of the hallway. The ch'i will flow from one mirror to the next, slowing down and oscillating down the hallway, rather than gaining speed as it races toward the end.

Avoid clutter. This slows and constricts the ch'i, making it stagnant and ineffective. Ch'i also stagnates in dark or unused areas. Keep your apartment well lit. Allow plenty of light and air into rooms, such as guest bedrooms, that are not used regularly.

Look for any internal shars that may exist inside your apartment. Examples include sharp edges and corners of furniture, a square-shaped pillar, or overhead beams. You may be able to move some furniture to eliminate the effects of such shars. Potted plants or mirrors can be used to remedy the effects of a pillar, and two bamboo flutes suspended from a beam eliminate its harmful effects.

Try to avoid spending any time sitting or working directly under overhead beams, and arrange your furniture so that your guests are not forced to sit directly under them.

Single-level apartments are better from a feng shui point of view than split-level or two-story apartments. The staircase should not be directly in front of the main door. This is because the ch'i gets confused when it comes into the apartment, not knowing which way to go. Also, the people who occupy the upstairs bedrooms are likely to come indoors and head directly to their bedrooms, rather than spend time with the other occupants of the apartment.

With split-level apartments, make sure that the kitchen and dining areas are higher than the living room. If the living room is on a higher level, your guests will take all of the good ch'i away with them when they leave.

All the rooms should be well proportioned, with no rooms seeming overly large at the expense of others. Ideally, the rooms should be square or rectangular in shape. L-shaped rooms give the impression that something is missing. The angle created that points into the room also creates a shar. The remedy for this is to hang a mirror on each side of the offending shar to symbolically make it disappear.

Living rooms should be close to the main entrance, with the kitchen and bedrooms farther away. This provides peace, harmony, and security. The residents can sleep soundly at night, away from any sounds that may be coming from outside the front door. The doors leading to the bathrooms, toilets, and bedrooms should not be visible from the front door.

Kitchens and bathrooms should not be sited in the center of the apartment. This is the "good luck" location and should be reserved as an area for all the people living in the apartment to use. Consequently, it is the perfect position for part of the living room or a family room.

In the next chapter we will determine the best place for each room according to your personal trigram.

5

Positive and
Negative Locations

In every apartment there are four positive and four negative locations, which are determined from your personal trigram. These locations are derived from the magic square found on the back of Wu's tortoise all those thousands of years ago, and are determined by your personal trigram.

The Positive Locations

Prime

The Prime location is excellent and is always the same as the direction toward which the house or apartment sits. In the East it is commonly referred to as **Fu Wei,** which means "good life." This location is the perfect position for bedrooms and doors.

Health

The Health location is also good, and relates to health, vitality, and friends. It is frequently referred to as **T'ien Yi,** which means "doctor from heaven." This is because activating this location is likely to help even prolonged illnesses that medical doctors have had problems in curing.[1] This location is excellent for the dining room and the master bedroom. This location can be stimulated with hanging crystals and wind chimes to help family members who are ill.

Longevity

The Longevity location is related to peace, harmony, and good health. It also plays a major part in ensuring harmonious family relationships. It is an excellent location for the bedrooms of older family members. This location can be stimulated with crystals and mirrors when the family is having problems among themselves. Stimulating this area helps relieve such difficulties and also helps resolve marital problems.

Prosperity

Many feng shui practitioners consider the Prosperity location the most auspicious position of all. It relates to forward progress, financial success, vitality, and exciting opportunities. It is a good location for the front door, kitchen door, master bedroom, study, and any other area where financial matters are dealt with. This is the worst position for the bathroom and toilet, because the water used in these rooms represents financial opportunities being flushed away. The Prosperity location is the perfect position for a desk where the family accounts are paid. This position should be kept well lit and stimulated with crystals and items that relate to your personal element. This is because it is believed that you will ultimately become wealthy if this area is kept activated.

In the East, many people orient their beds toward the Prosperity location, and also travel to work in this direction.

The Negative Locations

Death

The other name for this location is **Chueh Ming,** which means "total catastrophe." This location is related to accidents, illnesses, and other misfortunes. Not surprisingly, this is considered the worst location in the house. It is believed that if your front door faces this direction you and your family will suffer ill health and will also risk losing your money and good reputation. All of the negative locations are good places for the toilet, because the negative ch'i can be symbolically flushed away.

Disaster

The Disaster location is frequently known as **Ho Hai,** which means "accidents and danger." This generally refers to delays, frustrations, and small losses, rather than major disasters. Your bed should not point toward this direction because you will suffer frequent small mishaps if it does. The Disaster location is a good place for the storeroom, pantry, or toilet.

Six Shar

The Six Shar location is also known as **Lui Shar,** which means "six deaths." It relates to procrastination, scandal, and loss. It is also connected with legal and health problems. It is a good location for the kitchen and toilet.

Five Ghosts

The Five Ghosts location relates to fire, theft, and financial difficulties. It is believed that you could suffer from fire and theft if your front door faces this direction. This location is, like the Disaster location, a good place for a storeroom or toilet.

These locations are determined by the trigram of your apartment. The following lists describe the positive and negative locations for each trigram.

Chien House

A Chien house sits toward the northwest.

The Prime location is northwest.

The Health location is northeast.

The Longevity location is southwest.

The Prosperity location is west.

The Death location is south.

The Disaster location is southeast.

The Six Shar location is north.

The Five Ghosts location is east.

K'un House

A K'un house sits toward the southwest.

The Prime location is southwest.

The Health location is west.

The Longevity location is northwest.

The Prosperity location is northeast.

The Death location is north.

The Disaster location is east.

The Six Shar location is south.

The Five Ghosts location is southeast.

Ken House

A Ken house sits toward the northeast.

The Prime location is northeast.

The Health location is northwest.

The Longevity location is west.

The Prosperity location is southwest.

The Death location is southeast.

The Disaster location is south.

The Six Shar location is east.

The Five Ghosts location is north.

Tui House

A Tui house sits toward the west.

The Prime location is west.

The Health location is southwest.

The Longevity location is northeast.

The Prosperity location is northwest.

The Death location is east.

The Disaster location is north.

The Six Shar location is southeast.

The Five Ghosts location is south.

Li House

A Li house sits toward the south.

The Prime location is south.

The Health location is southeast.

The Longevity location is north.

The Prosperity location is east.

The Death location is northwest.

The Disaster location is northeast.

The Six Shar location is southwest.

The Five Ghosts location is west.

K'an House

A K'an house sits toward the north.

The Prime location is north.

The Health location is east.

The Longevity location is south.

The Prosperity location is southeast.

The Death location is southwest.

The Disaster location is west.

The Six Shar location is northwest.

The Five Ghosts location is northeast.

Chen House

A Chen house sits toward the east.

The Prime location is east.

The Health location is north.

The Longevity location is southeast.

The Prosperity location is south.

The Death location is west.

The Disaster location is southwest.

The Six Shar location is northeast.

The Five Ghosts location is northwest.

Sun House

A Sun house sits toward the southeast.

The Prime location is southeast.

The Health location is south.

The Longevity location is east.

The Prosperity location is north.

The Death location is northeast.

The Disaster location is northwest.

The Six Shar location is west.

The Five Ghosts location is southwest.

These locations can also be used as directions whenever you are doing something important. For instance, if you are a Chen, you would benefit by facing east, north, southeast, or south when making important decisions. (Chen belongs to the East Four Houses and these directions are the best directions for all members of this group, no matter what an individual's trigram is.) Gamblers in the East prefer to face their Prosperity direction when gambling, in the belief that this will bring them good luck. The Prosperity direction is determined by the individual trigram, rather than by a grouping of houses.

Determining the Locations in Your Apartment

We determine the different locations by superimposing a three-by-three magic square over a plan of the apartment. Obviously, this is easier if your apartment is square or oblong in shape than it is if your apartment is L-, T-, or U-shaped. In some instances it is better to divide the apartment into smaller sections and place a magic square on top of each. In fact, you can even do this exercise one room at a time, if you wish. Bedrooms are commonly evaluated in this way to determine the best position for the bed.

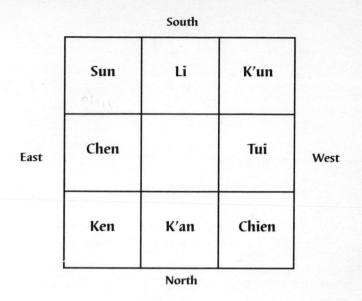

South

Sun	Li	K'un
Chen		Tui
Ken	K'an	Chien

East   West

North

Figure 5A: The Latter Heaven Sequence

The magic square is constructed with the eight trigrams placed in their correct positions. Figure 5A shows the correct position for each trigram according to the Latter Heaven Sequence. Figure 5B shows the placement for a Chen apartment.

In Figure 5C we have placed the magic square over a Chen apartment.

We can now interpret the plan of the apartment. A Chen apartment sits toward the east and faces the west. The front door is in the Disaster location, which is in the southwest. However, the door opens to the west. With the main

East

Ken 6 Shar	**Chen** Prime	**Sun** Longevity
K'an Health		**Li** Prosperity
Chien 5 Ghosts	**Tui** Death	**K'un** Disaster

North   South

West

Figure 5B: The Magic Square for a Chen Apartment

entrance in the Disaster location, the occupants will have more than their share of small mishaps and problems. The front door opens directly into a large living room. This provides a good glimpse of the interior of the apartment, but it gives the occupants no privacy from unexpected visitors. A screen near the front door would allow a large enough view of the interior and would also provide a degree of privacy for the occupants.

The living room is made up of the Death (west), Disaster (southwest), Prosperity (south), and Good Luck (center) areas of the apartment. The Prosperity location would

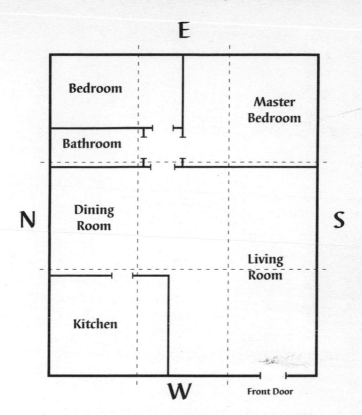

Figure 5C: Magic Square superimposed on apartment floor plan

make a perfect place for a desk where the family accounts could be paid. The Good Luck area is perfectly sited, because it is the location for family members to communicate and enjoy each other's company. The Death and Disaster locations are both negative positions and would make a better position for the bathroom than the living room. Fortunately, the front door is in the Disaster rather than Death location. If it had been in the Death location, the occupants would have ultimately lost everything. The Disaster location is related to disputes and disagreements. This would be the worst position in the room for a couch and chairs, because the people using them would argue and squabble all the time. (The Good Luck location is the best place in this living room for comfortable chairs and sofas.)

The kitchen is in the Five Ghosts location (northwest). Since this location relates to fire, the residents will have to take special care in this kitchen with all electrical and heating appliances.

The dining room joins onto the living room and is in the Health location (north). This is an excellent placement for the dining room; people eating here will enjoy good company and excellent health.

The master bedroom is in the Longevity location (southeast). This is an excellent location that gives the occupants peace, harmony, and a long life. It is well away from the front door, which is also good from a feng shui point of view.

The Prime location (east) is taken up with a third of the master bedroom, part of the second bedroom, and the small hallway. This is a good location for beds and doors. If possible, the occupants should place their beds in this part of their respective bedrooms. The hallway contains three doors, which is good. However, the doorway to the master bedroom is directly opposite the doorway to the bathroom, which is not good, because negative ch'i could drift into the bedroom. The remedy for this is to keep the bathroom door closed.

The Six Shar location (northeast) contains two-thirds of the spare bedroom and the bathroom. This is the perfect location for the bathroom, but is negative as far as the bedroom is concerned. The occupant of this room would be likely to put off making decisions and could become involved in scandal. Fortunately, one-third of the room is in the Prime location and the occupant could remedy the negative effects of the Six Shar location by sleeping with his or her head in the Prime location.

Aspirations of the Pa-kua

Another way of evaluating apartments, which is extremely popular in Hong Kong, where most people live in apartment buildings, is known as the **Aspirations of the Pa-kua.** It is controversial because it is part of the Compass School of feng shui but does not use a compass.

The same three-by-three magic square is overlaid on the apartment, in the same way as for the Eight Locations method. However, because the compass is not used, the front door or main entrance to the apartment is always placed on the bottom of the magic square.

There are nine different areas of the apartment that have to be examined (Figure 5D).

Wealth

The Wealth location is diagonally as far to the left of the front door as it is possible to go and still remain inside the

Wealth	Fame	Marriage
Family		Children
Knowledge	Career	Mentors

The main entrance is always on this side of the square

Figure 5D: The Aspirations of the Pa-kua

apartment. This area relates to money, finances, and abundance. If you want to attain these things, you need to activate the wealth area of your apartment. Increase the amount of light to encourage the ch'i into this part of your apartment. Crystals also encourage the ch'i in and reflect it in every direction. Place something metallic in this part of the house, also, because metal relates to money. An aquarium is also beneficial because water also relates to money in feng shui, and fish relate to success and achievement. Do not use an aquarium if you belong to the fire element, because water puts out fire. Instead, use ornaments of red fish to symbolize the fire element and to act as silent affirmations. Have something that precedes your personal element in the Productive Cycle of Elements in this area as well. Finally, you also need something that relates to your personal element in this area. All of these things will help to activate the wealth area of your home.

Fame

The Fame location comprises the middle third of the back part of the apartment, in between the Wealth and Marriage areas. Fame, in this instance, means increasing one's standing or reputation in the community. However, you can also activate this area if you want to become famous.

Again, we do this by increasing the light in this part of the apartment. We can also hang up crystals and place something that relates to our personal element in this area. It is a good idea to hang up a picture of yourself in this area as well. You should also display in this location any certificates, awards, or trophies you may have been awarded or earned.

Marriage

In the modern world, the Marriage location relates not only to marriage, but to all close, personal relationships. If you are looking for such a relationship, or want to improve your existing relationship, you should activate this area. Increase the light to activate the ch'i. Use crystals and have some attractive objects that relate to your personal element and that of your partner, if you have one. Photographs of the two of you together are also beneficial. If you are looking for a relationship, illustrations showing couples hand in hand, perhaps walking along a deserted beach, will help to activate this location. Anything that you consider to be romantic can be displayed in the Marriage sector.

Family

The Family location represents family in a wide sense of the word. It represents the people you are close to. It also represents health.

Activating this area encourages closer family ties and can be used when the family is arguing or is divided over some issue. This is a good location for family photographs and anything else that reminds you of close friends and loved ones. This area should also be activated when family members are having health problems.

Naturally, we need to increase the light in this part of the apartment to activate this area. We also need objects that relate to the personal element of the people we are trying to help. In the case of sick people, we want objects that relate to the element that comes before theirs in the Cycle of Production.

Children

The Children location is diagonally to the right of the front door, between the Marriage and Mentors areas. It can be activated in two ways.

If you are having problems with your children, you can activate this area by using objects that relate to the element that precedes theirs in the Cycle of Production. Naturally, you will also increase the light in this part of the apartment as well.

If you want to have children, this area is activated by increasing the amount of light and hanging up a crystal attached to a red ribbon. Healthy, young plants or freshly cut flowers can also be used. If you use flowers, make sure that they are thrown out as soon as they start to wilt, because dead and dying flowers create negative ch'i. Artificial flowers can also be used, but do not use dried flowers. This is because they have had all the water taken out of them, which is bad from a feng shui point of view. After all, feng shui means "wind and water."

Knowledge

The Knowledge area is on the same side of the apartment as the front door, and is as far to the left as it is possible to go. This location relates to learning, and is an excellent position for a library, study, or hobby room. Any type of work that requires mental stimulation will be performed better in this part of the apartment.

This area is stimulated in the usual way, by increasing the amount of light and by hanging crystals. It can also be activated by placing items that relate to whatever it is you are intending to learn in this area. For instance, if you were planning to learn a foreign language, you should study in this location, and you should also keep your instruction books and dictionaries here to help activate the room.

Career

The Career location is found in the middle of the apartment on the wall that contains the front door. If you are hoping to progress in your career, or perhaps find a new career, this area should be activated. Light, crystals, wind chimes, and objects that relate to your personal element can all be used. This is also a good place for your telephone, desk, and any office equipment, such as computers, fax machines, papers, and files.

Mentors

The Mentors location is on the right-hand side of the front door. An old saying states: "When the student is ready, the teacher will come." If you feel that you are ready, but the teacher has not yet arrived, you can speed up the process by activating this part of your apartment. Mentors can provide help, advice, and a shoulder to lean on in all areas of our lives. By activating this area, we encourage them to come and assist us.

We can activate this area in the usual ways. However, if we have a specific mentor in mind, and know his or her year of birth, we can also place something in this location that relates to this person's personal element.

The Mentors area also relates to travel. If you want to travel, you need to activate this area with a crystal and something that relates to your personal element. You also need to display pictures of the places you want to visit in this location.

Good Luck Center

The area in the center of the apartment is known as the Good Luck, or Spiritual, center. This area should be well lit to encourage the people who live in the apartment to communicate and spend time with each other. It is the perfect position in the apartment for a chandelier, because each crystal will reflect the ch'i out from the center to every corner of the apartment.

Directions

The Aspirations of the Pa-kua are not restricted by the walls of your apartment, but spread out endlessly. Consequently, if you are seeking wealth, you should look for it in the direction indicated by the placement of the Wealth location in your apartment. You can find a relationship in the same way by searching the area indicated by the placement of the Marriage area in your apartment.

If you want to progress in your career, you should head in the career direction every day when you go to work, even if your workplace is in a totally different direction. After driving a block or two, you can turn around and go in the correct direction. By doing this, you help activate your career.

We can evaluate the apartment in Figure 5C using the Aspirations of the Pa-kua.

The second bedroom and bathroom are in the Wealth location. This is the worst possible position for the bathroom, as all the wealth gets symbolically flushed away. The remedy for this is to keep the lid of the toilet down and to keep the door closed as much as possible. You might want to hang a mirror on the outside of the bathroom door to symbolically make the room disappear.

The occupant of the second bedroom can activate his or her room to benefit financially.

The Fame area utilizes part of each bedroom. If the occupants want to increase their reputation in the community, they can activate this part of their room.

The master bedroom is largely in the Marriage sector. This is the perfect placement, and the occupants of this room should enjoy a long, stable, and loving relationship. Naturally, they can also activate their bedroom to improve their relationship further.

The dining room is in the Family section. This is a good placement and the family would enjoy pleasant times together sitting around the dining room table.

The Children sector occupies about a quarter of the living room. Since this apartment does not have a family room, any children would naturally spend a great deal of time in this room. This part of the living room would be ideal for them to play in.

The kitchen takes up virtually all of the Knowledge area. Consequently, the occupants would enjoy studying at the kitchen table.

The Career area is largely in the living room, though a small portion is also in the kitchen. This part of the living room would be ideal to display any awards or trophies that are related to work. The Career part of the kitchen would be an ideal place for the telephone, fax machine, and anything else that relates directly to the occupants' careers.

The Mentors area is also in the living room. This is a good part of the room to entertain and to talk with older people and mentors.

In the above example, we have been restricted by the four walls. However, as you know, the Aspirations go out endlessly in every direction. Consequently, in this example, the occupants should seek wealth in the northeast direction, fame in the east, a relationship in the southeast, and so on.

Individual Rooms

We can use the Aspirations of the Pa-kua to evaluate a single room, and even something as small as a desk. In my travels in the Far East I have seen many desks with a small metal dish containing a few coins sitting in the Wealth position.

Let's assume that we are going to place the magic square over the master bedroom in Figure 5C. The bottom of the magic square has to be aligned with the main entrance. Consequently, the Wealth area of this room will be in the southeast corner.

Apartments can be of any shape. Consequently, many of them appear to be missing a piece when the magic square is superimposed over them. However, this is not necessarily the misfortune that it may first appear to be, because every room inside the apartment also contains a magic square. If your apartment is L-shaped and symbolically missing, for instance, the Wealth area, you can remedy that by activating the Wealth areas in different rooms inside your apartment.

The principles of feng shui may seem complex to begin with. The best way to learn them is to place a magic square over a plan of your own apartment and see how its interpretation compares to reality. You are likely to find that most of your apartment is already a positive environment, because we instinctively tend to do the right things. Using feng shui, you can do any necessary "fine-tuning" to make your apartment as perfect as possible. Once you have achieved that, you will be well on the way to a life of happiness, contentment, and abundance.

6

The Individual Rooms

The two most important rooms in an apartment from a feng shui point of view are the kitchen and the master bedroom. Of course, many apartments include everything except the bathroom inside one room. Even in this case, certain areas of the one-room apartment are used for specific purposes and can be examined individually. In the next chapter we will look at one-room, or studio, apartments in greater detail.

The Kitchen

Traditionally, the kitchen has always been the most important room in the home. This is because it contains the oven, which is considered the seat of the family's wealth. The quantity and quality of the food prepared in this room is important. Quantity is important because it enhances feelings of abundance, and quality because it benefits the family's health. Consequently, the refrigerator and pantry should be well stocked. In the East it is a matter of pride to have sufficient food in the house at all times to entertain unexpected guests.

The stove (or oven or microwave) should be placed in a position where the cook can easily see anyone who comes into the room. It is bad for the cook to work with his or her back to the door, as people walking in unexpectedly could cause a fright, and consequently affect the quality of the food. A mirror placed above or beside the stove can serve as a remedy if there is no alternative placement for the stove. This allows the cook to see anyone who comes into the room, and also symbolically doubles the amount of food coming out of the oven.

The stove should not face the front door, the bathroom door, or the entrance to the master bedroom. In studio apartments it should not face any bed.

The stove should be kept clean and work properly. Anything that does not work the way it should causes irritation and negative ch'i. If something does not work correctly in the kitchen, the seat of the family's wealth, it will also cause problems in the workplace.

Any drains and pipes should be concealed in both the kitchen and bathroom. This is because water represents money, and it is bad feng shui to watch it draining away.

Naturally, this room needs to be well lit to allow the ch'i in. This benefits the food as well as the people working here.

The Dining Room

The dining area should be close to the kitchen, but as far away as possible from the front door. This is because it is believed that if your guests can see the front door from the dining room table they will eat their meal and then leave. A screen can act as a remedy to conceal the door, if necessary.

The dining room needs to give the impression of spaciousness. It is important that people can get up from their places at the table without being restricted by walls or furniture. You can have as much furniture as you wish in the dining room, just as long as it does not restrict the movements of the people sitting at the table.

Round tables are believed to be the most conducive to conversation. However, square, oblong, oval, and pa-kua (eight-sided) shaped tables are all acceptable. It is better for square and oblong tables to have slightly rounded corners to eliminate any potential shars.

Mirrors serve two purposes in the dining area. They make the room appear larger, creating feelings of spaciousness. They also symbolically double the amount of food being served, giving feelings of abundance and well-being.

The dining room needs to be well lit to encourage the ch'i in. A candle-lit dinner is fine as long as sufficient ch'i has been allowed in beforehand.

The dining room should feel spacious and welcoming. Naturally, this is good from your guests' point of view, but the Chinese have another reason, even more important, for this. They believe that if the dining room is confined and

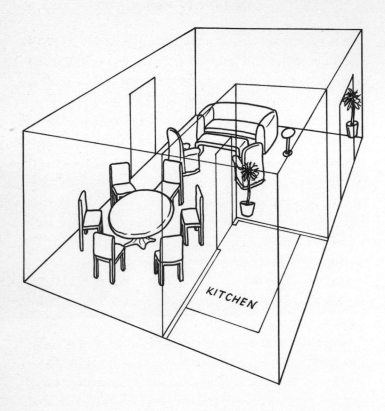

Figure 6A: Dining room and living room combined

restricted, your finances will also be constricted. Consequently, many Chinese people prefer the dining room to be part of the living room. This naturally creates a much larger room, with no walls to confine or restrict the fortunes of the occupants (Figure 6A).

The Living Room

The living room is an important room because it is where members of the family gather to relax and talk. It is also where we entertain our guests. Consequently, this room needs to be welcoming and comfortable.

The living room should reflect the personalities and interests of the occupants. A bookcase can display books on subjects that interest the occupants. Certificates and photographs can be hung on the walls or placed on tables. If an occupant collects something, these objects can make an attractive display. My mother used to collect antique ceramic chickens sitting on baskets. She displayed these in the living room of her apartment. They not only reflected her interest in ceramics, but also attracted beneficial ch'i, as the sun caught them for part of the day and reflected their cheerful colors around the room.

Ideally, the living room should be regular in shape. Mirrors can be used to rectify narrow or L-shaped living rooms. Mirrors on the long walls of narrow rooms can make them appear better balanced. Mirrors on either side of a sharp angle creating a shar can symbolically make it disappear.

The furniture should also reflect the personalities of the occupants. It should be comfortable and in keeping with the size of the room. The head of the family should sit in a position where he or she faces the main entrance to the room.

The Bedroom

Next to the kitchen, the bedroom is the most important room in the apartment. We all spend some eight hours a day sleeping, so the bedroom should be a safe, secure room where we can enjoy a deep, restful sleep.

The best location for the bedroom is as far as possible from the front door. In feng shui, the home is often divided into the outer and inner sections. The outer section includes the main entrance and contains the more public rooms, such as the living and dining rooms. The inner section contains the more private rooms, such as the toilet, bathroom, and bedrooms.

The alignment of the bedroom door is important. The entrance to the bedroom should not be in a direct line with the front door, because this takes away the security gained by locating the bedroom in the inner section of the apartment. Neither should the bedroom be in a direct line with the bathroom or kitchen, as odors and negative ch'i will waft into the bedroom.

The placement of the bed is extremely important. It should be in a position where the person lying in it can see anyone coming in through the door. The position diagonally opposite the door is usually the best one.

The eight locations can be used to help provide a suitable placement for the bed. You can choose whatever direction you want, depending on your personal ambitions. Usually, though, the bed is placed in the Health or Longevity locations. However, the aesthetics of the room also need to be taken into consideration. The bed should

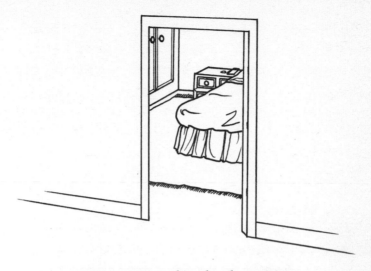

Figure 6B: Bed in death position

not be in a position that looks out of place or strange to anyone looking in. If you cannot place the bed in the position you want, you might be able to place it so that the head of the bed is pointing in the direction you want.

The foot of the bed should not face the door (Figure 6B). This is known as the "death" position, because it reminds the Chinese of the days when coffins were lined up in the courtyards outside the temples waiting for the right day to be buried. (Traditionally, corpses are also taken from the room feet first.)

Exposed beams are considered shars, no matter what room they are in. They are particularly bad in the bedroom if they cross over the bed. The person who sleeps in this bed is likely to suffer ill health in the part of the body that is directly below the exposed beam. For instance, if the exposed beam crosses over the person's chest, breathing problems or chest pains would be the likely result. If there is no alternative to the exposed beams, it is better if they run the length of the bed rather than across it.

The headboard of the bed should be in contact with a wall. However, it should not be placed directly under a window, because you will be exposed to drafts and also feel insecure. One side of the bed can contact a wall, if desired, for additional support. You should do this only if you want to sleep alone. If the bed is not touching a wall, it will lack support and the occupant will feel unsettled and find it hard to enjoy a good night's sleep.

Mirrors are beneficial everywhere in the apartment, but should be used carefully in the bedroom. They should not face the foot of the bed. This is because they can frighten the person sleeping in the bed if he or she wakes up during the night, because the person's reflection will be seen in the mirror and may look like a ghost. Mirrors in this position are also believed to put great strains on a relationship.

Mirrors should also not be directly opposite the door to the bedroom, because they send back the energies they receive, causing confusion to ch'i that tries to enter the room.

Mirrors can be extremely useful in the bedroom if the bed is situated in a position where the occupants cannot easily see anyone entering the room. In this case, a mirror can be used to allow the entrance, and any visitors, to be seen.

The occupants of the bed should have a pleasant view when they wake up in the morning. This could be an attractive outlook from the window, or perhaps a framed picture on the wall.

The window should allow fresh air and sunlight in during the day. However, it is not considered good to have direct sunlight on the bed itself. We want as much ch'i as possible to come into the bedrooms during the day. Most of the ch'i will come in through the door, but some also comes in through the windows. Many bedrooms are also used for other purposes, such as study. In these cases, extra ch'i is essential to provide the necessary vitality, enthusiasm, and stimulation to study or work.

Make sure that there are no external shars attacking the room through the windows. Heavy drapes provide a remedy if this is a problem. Shars can be a problem in the rooms of newborn babies. If your baby cries all the time, check for shars, both outside and inside the room. You will probably find the problem goes away once the shars have been rectified.

Dressing tables, bureaus, and chests of drawers should not be placed next to the bed because they are believed to disrupt the flow of ch'i.

The wallpaper and carpet in the bedrooms should harmonize with the occupant's personal element. The element preceding theirs in the Productive Cycle of Elements is also good. In fact, the preceding element is better for children's rooms than their personal element.

The Toilet

Whenever possible, toilets should be situated next to an outside wall of the apartment and be as inconspicuous as possible. They should be in the negative areas of the apartment. If it is located in the wealth, fame, or career sectors, for instance, the toilet "flushes" away the occupants' opportunities. Obviously, it is not practical to change the position of the toilet if you are already in the apartment. The remedies are to keep the seat down and the door closed. It is also a good idea to have a mirror on the outside of the toilet door to symbolically make the room disappear.

The toilet should not be in the center of the apartment. In this location, the negative ch'i produced will spread to every part of the apartment.

Toilets are intended to be inconspicuous; therefore, they should not be overly large. It is better to have a separate room for the bathroom. This is not possible in many apartments. If the two rooms are combined, separate them with a half wall to provide a degree of privacy and to dissipate the negative ch'i.

The Bathroom

The toilet and the bathroom represent the occupants' financial position because they are places where water (money) is used. Consequently, these rooms should not be visible from the front door or directly face the master bedroom. Neither should they be in the Wealth position.

The worst position for the bathroom is in the center of the apartment. In this location it will send negative ch'i to every part of the house. The remedy for this is to have a full-length mirror on the outside of the door, and two mirrors that reflect each other inside the bathroom itself. Mirrors on all four walls are even better.

The bathroom should be well lit and well ventilated. The colors should be delicate to maintain domestic harmony. Large mirrors are good in this room, but avoid mirror tiles. They create a netting effect that constricts the money flow.

Naturally, the bathroom and toilet should be kept scrupulously clean. Leaking taps and pipes indicate money slipping away. Problems should be repaired as soon as they occur.

En Suite Bathrooms

En suite bathrooms have become very popular in recent years and are frequently featured when a house or apartment is advertised for sale. Unfortunately, according to the principles of feng shui, there should be a clear division between the bathroom and bedroom, and therefore en suites are not recommended because they send negative ch'i into the bedroom. If your apartment contains an en suite bathroom, keep the door closed at all times.

Your apartment may contain all or most of the above rooms. However, particularly if your apartment is a small one, most of the above rooms will be combined. We will look at studio apartments in the next chapter.

7

Studio Apartments

Studio apartments consist of a main room, a kitchen or kitchenette, and a bathroom. However, I have been in a number of studio apartments where the bathroom was a communal one, shared with the occupants of other studio apartments on the same floor of the building.

Some of these apartments are extremely small and there is a tendency to have too much furniture, which constricts the smooth flow of ch'i around the apartment. Clutter is another major problem with small apartments, and the occupants need to be well organized and disciplined to keep everything in its proper place.

The best shapes for studio apartments are square, oblong, or L-shaped. It is unusual for an L-shape to be considered positive in feng shui. However, in this instance, it almost creates another room to serve as a bedroom or dining area.

Use either the Aspirations of the Pa-kua or your personal trigram to determine the positive and negative locations.

With a small studio apartment, I would be more inclined to use the Aspirations, though I would also refer to the trigrams to ensure that the apartment belonged to the same grouping as I do.

The most important placement in a studio apartment is the position of the bed. Once this has been decided, the rest of the room can be arranged around it. You may be fortunate and have two or three different positions that would suit the bed. In this case, you can choose the placement according to the eight locations or the Aspirations of the Pa-kua. It is more usual, however, especially in very small apartments, to find that there is only one practical place to put the bed.

The bed should feel protected. You may wish to have a moveable screen around it, or perhaps use a bookcase or some other furniture for symbolic protection. The bed should make contact with a wall, and the feet should not directly face the entrance to the apartment. The bed should not be hemmed in by walls or other furniture. I once spent a few nights sleeping in a bed that was in an alcove, making contact with the walls on three sides. I felt confined and restricted, even though the bed was of normal size. Anyone who slept in this bed for any length of time would experience restrictions and limitations in their own life.

If the apartment has a sloping ceiling, the bed should be placed close to the highest point. The ch'i gets more and more restricted the lower the ceiling becomes. Both sloping ceilings and exposed overhead beams affect the movement of the ch'i in a negative way and should be avoided if possible.

Many apartment dwellers use the bed as a couch during the day. In this case, the bed should be made to appear as much like a couch as possible. You might use a brightly colored cover and large cushions. If the bed is not being used during the day, you might want to use a screen to shield it from view.

If the kitchen area is also part of the single room, you may also want to screen it off when it is not being used.

Place the table where it will receive plenty of light. This is cheerful and is especially important if it is used as a work table as well as a dining table. Make sure that there is room around the table. We want a feeling of spaciousness around us when we work or eat.

The couch or sofa should be placed in an area that feels warm and comfortable. You should be able to see the front door from wherever you sit. If you will be using the couch a great deal, align it so that you can see the front door without turning your head.

Once the bed, table, and couch have been placed, the rest of the furniture can be placed as you wish.

The apartment should give a feeling of balance and harmony. Consequently, you should give some thought as to how your different interests will be accommodated. Naturally, your apartment should reflect your personality and interests, even if you intend to live there for only a short while. Display photographs and other precious items where you and your guests can easily see them.

If you work and live in your apartment you will need to separate the working and living areas. A friend of mine who is trying to make a career as a Hollywood scriptwriter works at a desk with his bed out of sight behind him. He has a pleasant outlook from his window and is, in a sense, away from home when he writes. Once he has finished for the day, he puts a screen around the desk to hide his computer from sight. This means that when he is working, he is able to focus on his work, without being distracted by other things inside his apartment. When he is not working, the working area is made invisible, so that he can enjoy his leisure time without constantly being reminded of work. Incidentally, his desk is in the Fame area of his one-roomed apartment.

The Studio Apartment Test

Stand at the entrance to your apartment and look around, trying to see it through the eyes of someone who has not visited before. Ask yourself these questions:

- Does it look cluttered? If so, the ch'i will not flow smoothly and your health and good fortune will suffer. Find a home for everything, rather than letting the clutter accumulate on the floor or tables.

- Even though the apartment might be small, does it give the impression of space? Mirrors can be used to symbolically double the size of the room. It is particularly important to have space around the bed and table.

- Is there sufficient light, particularly around the entrance, to encourage the ch'i in? Most of the ch'i comes in through the main door. This area needs to be kept well lit to encourage the ch'i and to make your apartment feel warm and welcoming.

- Are there any dark or gloomy corners? Stagnant and negative ch'i can gather in dark areas. Increase the light and hang crystals to encourage beneficial ch'i to visit these areas.

- Do you feel relaxed once you are inside? Your apartment is your home. It should be the place where you feel totally relaxed and at ease. You should be able to leave all the cares of the world behind you when you close the door. If you do not feel like this, you will have to take steps to improve the feng shui of the apartment to make it feel like "home."

- Is the color scheme attractive? Ideally, the color scheme should relate to your personal element. You will never feel totally at home, for example, if you belong to the fire element but live in an apartment with blue walls (which relates to water).

- Do you have on display some personal objects that reflect your interests? Many years ago, I spent several months living in a small apartment in Glasgow. The apartment was bleak and unattractive, but it became "home" for me just as soon as I displayed some brass rubbings I had made. When I arrived home from work they were the first thing I saw, and immediately reminded me of the pleasant times I had enjoyed visiting country churches looking for monumental brasses.

- Can you see the front door from your bed, and from where you normally sit and relax, without turning your head more than forty-five degrees? I am sure you know the expression "stabbed in the back." If you sit with your back to the door, you are symbolically unprotected and lacking in support, even in a small apartment where you live on your own. You subconsciously feel more in control when you can see the main entrance.

- Are there any shars attacking your main entrance or windows? If so, use feng shui remedies to eliminate them. A pa-kua mirror is the most effective way of eliminating outside shars. Wind chimes or hanging crystals are also effective for this.

- Have you activated the areas of your apartment that you wish to improve in your own life? If you want to learn more about some subject, place something that represents this area of interest in the Knowledge area. If you desire a relationship, put up something that represents this to you in the Marriage area. Increase the light in the areas that are of special interest. Look after these areas. Keep them dusted and clean.

As you can see, a one-room apartment is feng-shuied in exactly the same way as a large apartment or house. Instead of using individual rooms, separate areas are created for different purposes.

I have been in many studio apartments that feel much more comfortable, welcoming, and spacious than much larger apartments where no thought has been given to feng shui.

Some years ago, someone told me that he would never be wealthy as he lived in just one room, hemmed in and restricted by the four walls. As long as he felt that, his statement was true. However, if he had paid some attention to the feng shui of his apartment, particularly as far as enhancing the Wealth sector was concerned, he would have enjoyed feelings of abundance and ultimately made all the money he desired.

The size of the apartment has no bearing on health, wealth, or happiness. If you arrange your belongings in the correct way, even the smallest of apartments can become a safe haven that brings you everything you desire.

8

Conducting a Feng Shui Evaluation

Now that you know the basics of feng shui, you will find yourself using it whenever you visit a place for the first time. I usually receive an intuitive feeling for the room or home before mentally looking at the different locations. I find it fascinating that, although most people arrange their apartments without any knowledge of feng shui, they generally manage to get it about ninety-five percent right. Most of my consultation work involves fine-tuning rather than major adjustments.

An example of this occurred a short while ago. Bob and Linda are friends of mine. They had recently married and were contemplating buying a ground-level apartment in a small condominium. They asked me to come and have a look at it with them before they made their final decision.

Bob was born on December 3, 1968, which meant that his personal trigram was K'un. Linda was born on September 19, 1972, and had a personal trigram of Ken. This meant that they both belonged to the West Four Houses group and would be happiest in an apartment that sat toward the northwest, southwest, northeast, or west.

I was pleased to see that the apartment they were considering sat toward the northeast (Figure 8A). This was an excellent start.

We went up a curving path to the front door. There were no obvious shars affecting the main entrance, and there was a glimpse of a nearby river. This was a positive sign, because water in front of the property gave the opportunity for financial progress. They would have a much better view of the river if they cut a hedge back.

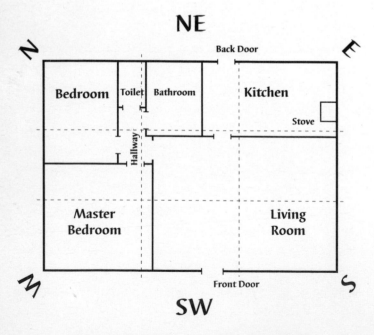

Figure 8A: Bob and Linda's apartment

The front door opened directly into a spacious living area. It was bathed in afternoon sun and was warm and inviting. From the front door I could see the kitchen and the back door. I could also see a sliding door that led through to the bedrooms. It is not good to see the back door from the main entrance, as the ch'i will come in and immediately leave through the back door. It is also a negative factor to see the kitchen from the front door, because your guests immediately think of food. However, it is an easy matter to keep this door closed when the kitchen is not being used. This effectively eliminates both problems.

The sliding door leading to the bedrooms was in the Wealth location of the living room. It would be a good idea for Bob and Linda to keep this door closed as well to hold the wealth inside the room.

The front door was well lit and the living room was like a magnet in attracting the ch'i indoors.

The kitchen was a good size and contained ample room for a table and chairs if Bob and Linda desired. The kitchen also contained ample bench space, but the placement of the oven meant that whoever used it would have his or her back to anyone entering the room. This could be solved by hanging a mirror above or beside the stove.

We went through the small hallway to the master bedroom. It was a good size, but felt cold and dark because the only windows were on the northwest side. This meant that it received virtually no sunlight. Bob and Linda would have to hang up a crystal and increase the light to encourage the ch'i into this room.

More seriously, the entrance of the bedroom immediately faced the entrance to the toilet. This meant that negative ch'i would waft straight into their bedroom. The remedy for this is to keep the door leading to the toilet shut.

The second bedroom faced north and was also cool. The difference in temperature between the warm living room and kitchen and the two bedrooms was incredible. The blinds would have to be raised in this room every morning to take full advantage of the sun.

It was good to see separate rooms for the toilet and bath. This gives the users more privacy and helps to dissipate the negative ch'i.

All in all, it seemed to be a very pleasant apartment with few defects, all of which could be remedied with just a little thought and effort.

I then drew up a plan of the apartment and superimposed a magic square on top to allow me to work out the Aspirations of the Pa-kua.

The Wealth location consisted of two-thirds of the second bedroom, a good third of the hallway and most of the toilet. The toilet was the most negative aspect of this placement, because all the wealth of the family would be "flushed" away. However, the dark, cold second bedroom was also negative because it tended to discourage rather than attract the beneficial ch'i.

The remedy for all this is to keep the toilet door closed. Bob and Linda should place a large, preferably full-length mirror on the outside of the door. Mirrors should also be placed on two opposing walls inside the toilet room to symbolically make the room disappear. In fact, mirrors on all four walls would be even better.

Light and warmth should be encouraged in the bedroom. Hanging a crystal from a red ribbon would help attract the ch'i, as would increasing the amount of light. The curtains should be pulled in the early morning to make the most of the morning sun.

In addition, something should be done in the bedroom to encourage prosperity. Bob belongs to the earth element and Linda is water. The element between these in the Cycle of Production is metal. Metal relates to money, and is particularly fortuitous for this couple because it also remedies the fact that earth and water oppose each other in the Cycle of Destruction. Bob and Linda should have an attractive metal object in this room to enhance their Wealth prospects. This could be a simple ornament, or it may be something more specifically related to money, such as a series of Chinese coins, joined together with red thread, hanging on the wall.

A fish tank would also prove beneficial in this room. However, as the room is dark and cold, it might be better to place the aquarium in the Wealth position of the living room where it would be noticed and admired.

The Fame position was taken up with the bathroom and a quarter of the kitchen. These are both places where water is used, which effectively means that the couple's reputation in the community would be drained away.

The remedy for this situation is to encourage the ch'i to rise away from the pipes and drains. Crystals can do this, and wind chimes should be hung near the back door, which is also in the Fame location. The wind chimes could be yellow, brown, blue, or black. (This is because Bob belongs to the earth element, and Linda to water.)

Incidentally, the presence of a back door is extremely good. In feng shui, a home without a back door is considered dangerous because there is only one way in and out. Many apartments have only one entrance. One of the reasons that this particular apartment appealed to Bob and Linda was that it had a back door.

The Marriage sector comprises the two-thirds of the kitchen that contains the oven, which is the seat of the family's good luck and fortune. This is not usually the best placement for the Marriage sector, but because the kitchen is a large one, Bob and Linda would be likely to spend many happy hours sitting at the kitchen table talking with each other.

However, they do not want their relationship to disappear with the water down the drain. Consequently, they should include in this room some of the things that represent love and romance to them. This could include photographs of the two of them, birthday cards, love letters, and pictures of romantic scenes.

The Family position comprises a third of the master bedroom, a third of the second bedroom, and two-thirds of the hallway. This area relates to the health and well-being of loved ones, and is well placed because attention can be paid to these matters here.

The Children location occupies a quarter of the living room. Bob and Linda are not planning a family at this stage, so will not activate this area. (If they had wanted children, they could have hung up photographs of young family members, and displayed toys or anything else that reminded them of children.)

The Knowledge sector takes up two-thirds of the master bedroom. This is a better place for books, files, papers, and office equipment than it is for sleeping. However, this could be a good room for study. Linda is halfway through an interior decorating course and would find this bedroom a good place in which to learn.

The Career location takes up the quarter of the living room that includes the front door. This would make a good location for a desk, telephone, and anything else that related to their respective careers. It is already well lit, but could be activated more with crystals if desired. (Linda is planning to purchase a chandelier for the center of the living room, which would help the ch'i of the entire apartment, and particularly the locations inside the living room.)

The Mentors sector takes up the final quarter of the living room. Linda is vitally interested in guardian angels and intends to activate this area with pictures and ornaments of angels.

This apartment is fairly standard in that it contains a mixture of good and bad locations. It would be impossible to find an apartment that was totally perfect, and the remedies required to improve the feng shui of this apartment are all minor.

However, before telling Bob and Linda the good news, I also did an evaluation using the eight locations.

The apartment sits toward the northeast, and belongs to the Ken trigram. It is the end apartment of an oblong building that also sits toward the northeast.

The positive directions are northeast (Prime), northwest (Health), west (Longevity), and southwest (Prosperity). The negative directions are southeast (Death), south (Disaster), east (Six Shar), and north (Five Ghosts).

The Prime location includes the bathroom and one quarter of the kitchen. This location is frequently referred to as the "good life" location, and is a good place for beds and doors. Unfortunately, we have water draining away in both rooms, and remedies will have to be used to eliminate the adverse effects. Additional light, crystals, and an aquarium all make ideal remedies.

The Health direction is northwest, which includes one-third each of the master bedroom and second bedroom, as well as two-thirds of the hallway. This is an excellent location for the master bedroom and, if the area is stimulated, it will bring good friends and excellent health to the occupants of the apartment.

The Longevity direction is to the west. This takes up two thirds of the master bedroom, and could not be bettered as it brings peace, harmony, happiness, good health, and a long life to the people sleeping in this room.

The Prosperity direction is the southwest. This occupies one-quarter of the living room and is the most fortunate direction in the apartment. This is a good placement for a desk where the family accounts are paid and investments made. The chandelier that Linda is planning to put in will make a noticeable difference to their ultimate prosperity. It is also the best location for the front door, which fortuitously is in this direction.

The first negative location is Death, which is in the southeast. This occupies one-quarter of the living room and is the worst location in the home. This would have been the perfect place for the toilet and bathroom. This direction is related to illness, accidents, and misfortune. Fortunately, the chandelier will send light to every part of this location, increasing the positive ch'i.

The Disaster direction is south. This occupies another quarter of the living room and is related to anger, disputes, and quarrels. Chairs and couches should not be placed in this part of the living room. This would make a good place for the television or stereo unit.

The Six Shar direction is east. This comprises two-thirds of the kitchen, which is well sited here.

The final direction is the Five Ghosts, which is north. This area is made up of two-thirds of the second bedroom, the toilet, and two-thirds of the hallway. The toilet is very well located here. However, the Five Ghosts direction is related to fire and theft. It is important that smokers not be allowed to smoke in this area, and that this part of the house be securely locked up each time the occupants leave the apartment.

I explained all of this to Bob and Linda and recommended that they buy the apartment. They are very happy in their new home. Linda had an instinctive feeling about where to place their furniture to allow the ch'i to flow through their apartment with as little interference as possible, and their apartment has a wonderful, welcoming feel to it.

Here is another example, this time a one-room apartment. Bruce is a former electrician who is back in school studying law. He consulted me because a former girlfriend had warned him about a shar inside his apartment. Bruce was born on July 4, 1972, which meant his trigram was K'an, one of the East Four Houses. His apartment shared the K'an trigram because it sat to the north.

Bruce's apartment was a single room in what had originally been a large mansion. The building is now very dilapidated and has been converted into about a dozen small apartments. All the other apartments use the main entrance to the building, but Bruce has his own entrance which leads into a long, dark passage. At the end of this hallway is his room (Figure 8B).

His girlfriend considered the long hallway to be a shar, because it was a straight line. This is true, but it is directed at a blank wall at the far end, so is not a true shar in that it does not directly affect Bruce. The main problem of a long hallway like this at the entrance is that the ch'i will come in, race down the hallway at great speed and rebound into the apartment. I suggested that he hang up two mirrors on each side of the hallway. This slows down the ch'i because it will head toward one mirror and then move on to the next mirror on the other side of the hall. Consequently, the ch'i will slow down and move in a wave-like manner down the hallway. As Bruce was concerned about what his girlfriend had said, I suggested he also hang a large mirror at the end of the passage to symbolically remove the shar.

Bruce owned a light fitting that contained several glass crystals. He had not hung it up because he intended to stay in the apartment for a short time only. I suggested that he hang it up beside the entrance to the main room of the apartment. This would attract the ch'i and cause it to bounce off in every direction. I also suggested that he install more lights along the hallway to make it brighter

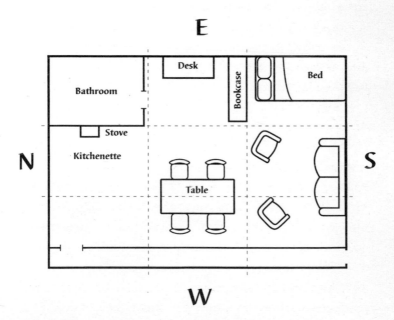

Figure 8B: Bruce's apartment

and more welcoming. This was particularly easy for Bruce to do because he used to make his living as an electrician.

The entrance to the main room was cheerful and gave a clear view of the apartment. Straight ahead was a small kitchenette area. Behind this was the bathroom. To the right, Bruce had a table and chairs and a lounge suite.

On the far wall, next to the bathroom, was his study area, which was separated from the bed by a bookcase. The room was welcoming and felt comfortable.

I began my analysis using the Aspirations of the Pa-kua. It is possible to do this on a room-by-room basis. Rather than place myself at the main entrance to the apartment, I worked from the doorway leading into Bruce's room.

From this perspective, the Wealth sector was completely missing, as this area was taken up with the bathroom. Bruce laughed when I told him this, as he is currently a struggling student, juggling three part-time jobs along with his studies.

All the same, I suggested that he place a mirror on both sides of the angle created by the bathroom. This also served another purpose. When Bruce worked at the oven, he had his back to the door. This meant that he was symbolically unprotected, even though he lived alone, and anyone coming in would have to walk along the hallway first. By placing a mirror in that position he would also be able to see anyone coming into the room without having to turn around.

Bruce's study area is located in the Fame sector. This is a good position, as he intends to make a name for himself as an attorney once he goes into practice.

The bookcase is also in a good position. It keeps Bruce's books where he can easily reach them while studying, and also separates the sleeping area from the work area.

Bruce's bed is in the Marriage sector. Bruce found this amusing, because he had recently finished a lengthy relationship and did not want another one at the moment. The single bed appeared to emphasize this. The only light in this area was a bedside lamp, which he turned on only when he wanted to read in bed. When he is ready for a new relationship, Bruce could easily activate this area with more light, a hanging crystal, and a romantic poster.

The kitchen area was in the Family sector. This is a good placement because Bruce is gregarious and loves to entertain. He is an excellent cook and spends a great deal of time in this part of the room, preparing meals for his guests. The only adverse part of this area was the placement of the stove, which could be easily remedied with a mirror, as mentioned earlier.

The Good Luck, or Spiritual, center was taken up by a table and chairs, which also spread into the Career sector. Bruce and his guests would enjoy sitting around the table, discussing a wide range of subjects. Since many of his guests were fellow students, much of this talk would relate to their studies and future careers.

Incidentally, Bruce instinctively did something that I frequently suggest to people who live on their own. Most people in this situation habitually sit in the same chair all the time, and the other chairs are not used. Bruce deliberately varied his seating position so that he could, as he put it, "have a different perspective on the world." The feng shui reason is not quite the same. When all the chairs are being used, you symbolically encourage visitors to call. When the chairs are not being used, you symbolically tell people to stay away.

Bruce's couch and two armchairs were situated in the Children and Mentors sectors. He felt they were perfectly sited there because his visitors varied. Some were playful, fun-loving types who responded to the Children's sector, but others were older friends who were, from Bruce's point of view, mentors. Both groups would feel happy in this part of the room.

I suggested that Bruce sit on the couch more frequently than in the armchairs. This is because he had a clear view of the room and the entrance from the couch. This put him in a commanding position.

The Knowledge area of the room was largely wasted, because it was the entrance to the room. Bruce had several piles of books around his desk. I suggested that he buy another bookcase and place it in the Knowledge sector.

The Career sector was partially occupied by the table and chairs. On the wall, though, Bruce had a photograph of his grandfather, who had been a judge. He had done this instinctively, but it was the perfect place to hang it, as it reminded him of the path he intended to follow.

The main problem with the apartment was clutter. Bruce was rather disorganized and there were papers and folders everywhere. This was easily remedied, though. The books were taken off the floor once he bought another bookcase.

This gave him room on the existing bookcase to store his files and papers.

Bruce was obviously highly intuitive and had done most things correctly. Once he made the changes I suggested, he found it easier to study and now has just one more year at law school to finish his degree.

I also used the eight locations to evaluate his apartment. This is done from the sitting position of the apartment, which was north.

The Prime location is in the north and comprised Bruce's kitchen area. This is a highly favorable location that would have made a good sleeping area. However, as Bruce loves working in his kitchen, this is a good placement for him.

The Health location is in the east. This is Bruce's study area. This location brings vitality and energy, both of which Bruce needs during the long hours he spends studying at his desk.

The Longevity direction is in the south, where Bruce has his couch and armchairs. This area provides peace and harmony, and ensures that Bruce's friends have an enjoyable time when they visit.

The Prosperity direction is the southeast. This is where Bruce has his bed. This would be the best location for Bruce's desk, and is largely wasted because he has the least light of all in this area. However, he is currently a student, and is paying more attention to his studies than he is to wealth. All the same, money is still required, and Bruce could activate this by increasing the amount of light in this part of the room. If he was concerned that doing this would also produce a relationship (as this is the Marriage sector using the Aspirations), he could use a small metal container holding a few coins to activate wealth rather than a relationship.

Bruce intuitively chose to sleep with his head pointing in the Prime direction. In this case, it would not have mattered if he had slept with his head at the other end of the bed, because then he would be pointing towards the Longevity direction, another positive placement. My only concern about his sleeping position was that he was not able to see anyone who came in the door, which he would be able to do easily if he slept at the other end of the bed. However, a mirror simply and effectively eliminated this particular problem.

The Death direction is southwest. This is where Bruce's main entrance is, and this sector also includes part of the entertaining area. This would have made an excellent location for the toilet, and is the worst possible location for the front door. Fortunately, although it is in this sector, the front door faces due south. If it had faced southwest, Bruce would have risked losing his money and reputation. When he increased the amount of light in the entrance, Bruce effectively limited the negativity of this direction.

The Disaster direction is west. This sector includes the middle section of the hallway and part of the dining area. This is related to arguments and disputes. Fortunately, Bruce has a light in this sector to encourage beneficial ch'i in. I suggested that he also hang a small crystal near the wall in this sector.

The Six Shar direction is northwest. This sector contains the doorway leading from the hallway into Bruce's main room. It relates to legal matters and bad health. The mirror at the end of the hallway and the light fitting that Bruce finally installed in this location act as good remedies. This area is also related to procrastination. Fortunately, this part of the apartment is used solely for entering and leaving the room. Bruce has no time to sit around and do nothing.

The Five Ghosts direction is northeast. This is where Bruce's bathroom is located. This is the perfect location for the bathroom and toilet. This area relates to fire and theft. Consequently, Bruce would have to ensure that the bathroom windows are securely closed and locked when he goes out.

Bruce was delighted with his feng shui analysis. He has bought some books on the subject and plans to study the subject when time allows. These books are on the bookcase in the Six Shar area. I doubt that Bruce will find time to study feng shui until he moves to a different apartment.

I hope these evaluations have shown you the benefit of using two different systems to evaluate an apartment. The Aspirations can be done quickly and easily with no special equipment. You need a compass and an accurate plan of the apartment to make the most of the Eight Locations method. Together, they allow you to analyze and evaluate your apartment and make any necessary changes.

9

Furniture Placement

You are now fully aware of the importance of the ch'i and how it should flow smoothly and effortlessly throughout the apartment. Any furniture has to be arranged to take account of this, as it can easily disrupt or block the smooth flow of ch'i. Large pieces of furniture are particularly prone to do this. The best place for these items is against the wall.

Recently, I was called in to feng shui the apartment of an elderly lady who lived on her own. Her small apartment was so full of furniture that I asked her if she was an antique dealer. It turned out that she had inherited furniture from a variety of relatives and had kept every piece. Although the furniture was beautiful, it created clutter in her apartment.

Rooms should have empty spaces as well as full ones. This provides a good balance of yin and yang energy. Some rooms have most of the furniture on one side, and this creates a feeling of tipping over or sinking (Figure 9A). The furniture should be placed in a way that makes the room appear balanced.

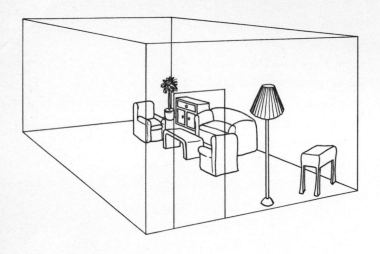

Figure 9A: An unbalanced room

It is a good idea to allow a certain amount of space around individual pieces of furniture as well, so that the ch'i can circulate. This applies even to beds. A friend of mine spent several months sleeping on a mattress in a friend's apartment. He was surprised to find that he suddenly had more energy and vitality as soon as he started sleeping on a bed again. It is essential for the ch'i to circulate under the bed, as well as around it, to allow the person sleeping on it sufficient rest.

The direction that the bed faces is also important. A bed facing the wrong direction can have a major adverse effect on relationships and careers. Your bed should face one of your positive directions for best results.

In the dining room, the table should be in proportion to the size of room. Many apartments do not have a separate dining room, and this is considered a good thing in feng shui. This is because the Chinese believe that if the dining room is completely enclosed, financial opportunities will be restricted. Consequently, a dining area that is part of the living room is good from a feng shui point of view.

The dining room, more than any other room, should not be cluttered with too much furniture. People sitting around the table should be able to get in and out without feeling restricted in any way.

Dining room tables are usually rectangular. These work well because most dining areas are also oblong in shape. Round, oval, and pa-kua shaped dining tables are also good choices. The host and hostess should sit at each end of a rectangular table. If there is just one host, it is a pleasant gesture to invite the guest of honor to sit at the end of the table that faces the main entrance to the room.

In the living room, none of the chairs or couches should have their backs pointing directly toward the main entrance to the room. Neither should they be located directly under any overhead beams or facing major shars.

Couches and chairs gain support from walls and benefit from having their backs to them. People never feel as comfortable when the back of the chair they are sitting in faces a door or window.

Chairs and couches should not be so close to each other that people sitting in them feel constricted. Coffee tables that are too close to couches and chairs can also produce the same effect. Chairs and couches should not be placed too close to the fireplace, because you want your guests to be warm rather than hot.

It is important that the head of the household sit in a position where he or she can see the main entrance to the room (Figure 9B). A position that is diagonal to the main entrance is known as the "command position" and lends authority and power to the person sitting there. In fact, the main entrance should be visible to as many people as possible. A strategically placed mirror can provide this view for people sitting with their backs to the door. It is a courteous gesture to offer the chair with the best view of the door to your guests. However, use it yourself when you are not entertaining. (Remember, though, to also use the other chairs from time to time, if you want to encourage guests to visit.)

The furniture should be arranged for comfort and ease of communication. Stiff, uncomfortable furniture creates feelings of unease and hinders relaxed conversations. Furniture arranged in semi-circular, circular, or pa-kua-shaped formations encourages communication. Triangular and L-shaped arrangements create a shar in the form of an arrow. However, this does not occur when the L-shaped arrangement is against two walls.

Place frequently used items where you can easily reach them. Favorite ornaments should be placed where they can be seen and enjoyed. Paintings and photographs should be displayed where they can be appreciated from both a sitting and standing position.

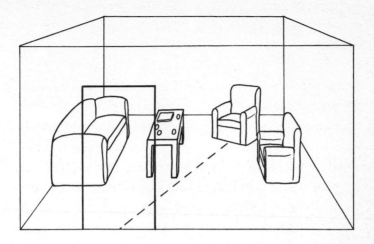

Figure 9B: The "command position"

Collections of items should be displayed in one or two areas, rather than throughout the house. It is better to create a feature rather than a feeling that items have been scattered carelessly around the apartment, creating clutter.

Mirrors can be placed almost anywhere. In the living room, they can be placed to reflect the entrance for people sitting with their backs to it. Above the mantelpiece is a common position for a mirror. Mirrors are related to water energy, because their surface reflects in the same way that water does. Consequently, a mirror above the fireplace balances the energy caused by the heat.

Lights can be used to brighten dark corners and to create a mood. There will be times when you will prefer subdued lighting, but generally you will want your rooms to be well lit. Lighting can be used to create atmosphere, but it is also used to encourage ch'i, and the general rule is to have rooms as well lit as possible.

It is a good idea to start arranging the room using the most important item of furniture first. In the bedroom, this will be the bed, of course. In the dining room, the table is obviously the most important item, as is the couch or sofa in the living room. Once you have found the ideal position for this piece of furniture, your other items can be placed in relation to it.

The center of the apartment is the good luck position. Every individual room also has a good luck center. Ideally, this area should be left free of furniture to allow the ch'i to circulate freely. The one major exception to this is the dining room. In this instance, the ch'i can still circulate freely under, over, and around the table.

10

Feng Shui Problems

One of the wonderful things about feng shui is that there is a remedy for just about everything. In my experience, the only problem that I have not been able to help someone with was a house located directly underneath high-tension electric power lines. There is increasing evidence that the electromagnetic fields that come from the electrical currents flowing through these high-tension wires cause a variety of potentially fatal diseases.[1] I advised this family to move to a new house.

Fortunately, that is an extreme case. Most of us can enhance the feng shui of our apartments by using remedies to eliminate shars and to improve the balance and harmony of our environment.

Obviously, the first thing to do is to protect yourself from any shars that might be directed at your apartment or the apartment building.

Shars travel only in straight lines. Consequently, they can be deflected in a variety of ways. For instance, if you own your own apartment, you might be able to change the angle of the front door to deflect a potentially damaging shar. This is an extreme remedy, of course, but it is effective when faced with a major shar, such as a large apartment building that is directly in front of your front door.

A less extreme remedy would be to build a wall, or plant trees or a hedge to hide the shar from view. In feng shui, a shar ceases to exist if you cannot see it. Trees take time to grow, of course, so you would also need to use a pa-kua mirror until the shar was hidden from view. Make sure that you choose evergreen trees with broad leaves. A single tree can become a shar in its own right, if any of its branches point directly towards your main entrance. Consequently, you should always plant a number of trees, rather than just one.

Incidentally, trees planted behind the apartment building provide a good form of support for everyone living inside.

The pa-kua mirror is a powerful feng shui remedy. Mirrors are normally passive and yin. However, a pa-kua mirror gains strength from the trigrams surrounding it, and are yang and aggressive. If placed just above the door, a pa-kua mirror will send the shar back where it came from.

Last year I saw some interesting decorations for front doors on sale in Hong Kong. They consisted of an attractive feng shui illustration, showing mountains, valleys, and streams. However, incorporated into the design was a pa-kua mirror to counter any shars. These decorations were attached to the front door, and looked extremely attractive. Unless you looked at them closely, you would not notice the pa-kua mirror.

After evaluating the main entrance to the apartment building, check the main entrance to your apartment.

Obviously, you cannot build a wall or plant trees if your apartment is several floors above the ground. However, you can use a pa-kua mirror to serve as a remedy. Do this if your main entrance faces sharp corners, elevators, escalators, or staircases heading downward.

The doors inside your apartment can be used to enhance your feng shui. You will remember that we used the shape of the pa-kua to give us eight directions. The direction that each door in our apartment faces has a specific meaning. Naturally, if you want to reap the benefits of a particular direction, you will have to use the door regularly and also enhance it to activate the ch'i.

A door facing south is related to the fire element and to fame. Use this door frequently if you want to increase your reputation and standing in the community. There are a number of ways in which you can activate this area. You can increase the light, perhaps with a feature spotlight. Alternatively, you could display something red, or use potted plants or freshly cut flowers.

A door facing southwest is related to the earth element and brings the potential for an excellent relationship. This area can be enhanced with ceramic or pottery objects, or anything that is red in color. A friend of mine used a bright red light by this door when she was looking for a new relationship. She is now married and expecting her first child.

A door facing west is related to the metal element and to children. This is an excellent direction for the doors of children's bedrooms to face. They can be activated by metal wind chimes, crystals, and porcelain or other ceramics.

A door facing northwest is related to the metal element, and to mentors and travel. This area can be activated with metal, ceramic and pottery objects, and crystals.

A door facing north is related to the water element and to your career. If you want to progress further in your field you should use this door as much as possible. You can also activate it by hanging a metal wind chime nearby (metal creates water). You could also have an aquarium or small indoor fountain in the vicinity of the door.

A door facing northeast is related to the earth element. It also relates to knowledge and learning. This direction is a highly positive one for a study or for children's bedrooms. It can be activated by bright lights or something red (because fire creates earth). Pottery and ceramics can also be used.

A door facing east is related to wood, as well as to family and close friends. It would be impossible to find a better direction for a door leading into the family room to face. This area can be enhanced with water, because water nurtures wood. Consequently, an aquarium or indoor fountain would enhance this location. Potted or hanging plants will also help activate this door.

A door facing southeast can bring financial rewards to anyone who uses it frequently. It is related to the wood element. You can enhance the effects of this door by using potted plants, cut flowers, or an aquarium.

It is better for doors to open onto the broader side of the room, and the door itself should be able to open so that it is parallel to the wall it is on.

Doors are there to be used. If you find that certain doors in your apartment are never used, you should either make a point of using them to keep them working for you, or symbolically make them disappear by hanging a mirror on them. Doors that are not used can cause bad luck. Consequently, if a member of the family is away and his or her room is shut off, you need to open and close it once or twice every day to keep it activated.

You may find that certain rooms in your apartment are less welcoming than others. This is likely to be because the yin and yang of the room are not in balance. Check to see that there is a balance of light and shade, furniture and space, and that the furniture is not all on one side of the room. The whole apartment should be checked for a yin-yang balance. There should be quiet, peaceful rooms as well as louder ones. Some rooms should be brightly lit, while others need a more subdued light.

You can also use the five elements to help harmonize and balance your apartment. Every element corresponds to one of the eight directions:

South	=	fire
Southwest	=	earth
West	=	metal
Northwest	=	metal
North	=	water
Northeast	=	earth
East	=	wood
Southeast	=	wood

You should keep these elements in mind when you decide to make changes to certain parts of your apartment. For instance, the southwest and northeast would be the worst directions in which to keep an aquarium because, in the Destructive Cycle of Elements, earth overpowers water.

Lights are an extremely important feng shui remedy. They can be used to illuminate dark corners where ch'i tends to stagnate. We have a dark entrance lobby, and keep the lights on in this area all the time to attract as much ch'i as possible into our home. Bright lights attract the ch'i, no matter where they are placed. However, it is more important to attract the ch'i into the main entrance than anywhere else.

Chandeliers and hanging crystals serve a number of purposes. Not only do they look attractive, but they also attract ch'i and then reflect it off in every direction. The best place for a chandelier is in the center of the apartment, which is the good luck location. Ch'i attracted to a chandelier in this location will spread to every part of the apartment. Chandeliers also work well in the south (where the element is fire) and the southwest and northeast (wood element) parts of the apartment.

Mirrors are probably used more than any other feng shui remedy. They are able to symbolically double anything they reflect. Consequently, they are very useful in the dining room for reflecting the food that is on the table. They can be used to reflect light and make rooms appear larger than they really are. This is particularly useful when the lobby area is small or unusually narrow. Mirrors can symbolically complete unusually shaped rooms to make them appear square or oblong. Mirrors can also be used to reflect a beautiful outdoor scene, effectively bringing it indoors.

The only place where mirrors should be used with care is in the bedroom. Mirrors should not face the bed, particularly from the bottom end. The traditional explanation for this is that it can cause the occupants a fright if they wake up in the night and see their reflection in the mirror. However, this placement is also often related to marital problems.

Mirrors should be as large as possible. Small mirrors symbolically cut off people's heads and feet.

Wind chimes make pleasing sounds in the breeze. This tells you that the ch'i is flowing. It is important to choose chimes that have hollow tubes, as the ch'i rises up through them. Wind chimes are extremely popular in the East because they are believed to bring good luck and money to their owners.

Wind chimes can be made from a variety of materials, such as metal, bamboo, glass, and ceramics. Metal wind chimes can be painted to represent any of the elements. Some feng shui practitioners say that wind chimes should be used outside only, but most agree that they can be used indoors as well. The west and northwest are good directions to hang metal wind chimes, because they relate to the metal element. Bamboo wind chimes should be hung in the east and southeast, because they represent the wood element. They can also be hung in the south, because wood creates fire. (However, do not hang metal wind chimes in the east or southeast, because metal destroys wood in the Destructive Cycle of Elements.)

Flowers are always a cheerful sight and encourage the ch'i. Potted plants and freshly cut flowers are the best for people in apartments. Remember that dead flowers create negative ch'i, so throw out cut flowers as soon as they start to fade. Artificial flowers can also be used, and make a good alternative for busy people. Make sure that your artificial flowers are kept dusted and clean, because you do not want them to create stagnant or negative ch'i. Dried flowers are not good from a feng shui point of view because all the water has been removed.

All other flowers are good, and the more colorful they are, the better. There are five flowers that have special meanings in feng shui, and are believed to be especially beneficial.[2]

> **The peony** represents love, wealth, and honor. Flowering peonies are believed to encourage wealth.
>
> **The chrysanthemum** is the flower of happiness and laughter. It symbolizes comfort and relaxation. Peonies and chrysanthemums are the most commonly seen flowers at the Chinese New Year celebrations.
>
> **White magnolias** and **orchids** represent femininity, good taste and serenity.
>
> **The lotus,** the sacred flower of the Buddhists, symbolizes purity. This is not surprising because the beautiful lotus rises from the mud and sits triumphantly on the surface of the water.

All plants create ch'i and help to bring harmony and balance into the home. The best locations for them are in the east, southeast, and north directions, because these relate to the wood and water elements.

Plants can also be used to eliminate the shars caused by sharp corners. Friends of mine have a climbing plant that encircles a square pillar located at the entrance to their living room. The plant is healthy and makes an attractive display, while at the same time making a potential shar disappear.

Aquariums and small indoor fountains can become a feature of a room, while at the same time increasing the wealth of the occupants. Water symbolizes wealth and abundance. Gently moving water also promotes calmness and serenity. However, you should not use water in the south part of your apartment, because fire and water do not get along. The opposite applies in the north. An aquarium or fountain in this location will help you progress more quickly in your career. The west and northwest are also good locations for an aquarium, because metal creates water. Likewise, the east and southeast are also positive, because water produces wood.

Stone, metal, ceramic, and glass animals are also used in feng shui. Fierce animals, such as lions, tigers, and birds of prey, are generally placed outdoors to provide symbolic protection for the building. This is why you sometimes see a pair of lions placed on each side of the main entrance to a building. Smaller, less fierce animals, such as tortoises and rabbits, are more commonly found indoors. (Tortoises represent longevity and rabbits, fertility.) My mother had a collection of chickens that gave her great pleasure. Small animals can be fun to collect, and provide symbolic protection for the home.

11

Conclusion

The goal of feng shui is to put balance and harmony into your life. You are unique. Your home is not exactly the same as anyone else's. The floor plan might be identical to someone else's, even the furniture could be the same, but you invest your home with your own personality. The way you arrange your furniture, your choice of decorations and ornaments, the way you display them, the amount of fresh air you allow in, and a host of other things make your apartment different from every other apartment.

The chances are that you are quite happy with the way you have your apartment arranged. There are probably a few things about your apartment that you would like to change, but by and large you are reasonably contented with it.

However, by using feng shui to "fine tune" what you have already done, you can become even happier with your home. Once you have done this, you will find that every aspect of your life will also improve, because you will be expressing this harmony and balance everywhere you go.

Take your time in making feng shui changes. It is better to make one change at a time. By doing this, you can evaluate what happens following a change. After a few weeks, make one more change. Then, a few weeks later, make another. By doing this, you will prove to yourself that feng shui works.

From now on, you will never look at space in the same way again. Your relationship to every environment you find yourself in will change for the better. Your life will improve in many subtle ways as you learn to bring more of the bountiful, beneficial ch'i into your world.

Make the most of this bountiful ch'i. Use it to create the life you want to live.

Appendix 1

Elements and Signs for the Years 1900 to 2000

Element	Sign	Year
Metal	Rat	Jan. 31, 1900 to Feb. 18, 1901
Metal	Ox	Feb. 19, 1901 to Feb. 7, 1902
Water	Tiger	Feb. 8, 1902 to Jan. 28, 1903
Water	Rabbit	Jan. 29, 1903 to Feb. 15, 1904
Wood	Dragon	Feb. 16, 1904 to Feb. 3, 1905
Wood	Snake	Feb. 4, 1905 to Jan. 24, 1906
Fire	Horse	Jan. 25, 1906 to Feb. 12, 1907
Fire	Sheep	Feb. 13, 1907 to Feb. 1, 1908
Earth	Monkey	Feb. 2, 1908 to Jan. 21, 1909
Earth	Rooster	Jan. 22, 1909 to Feb. 9, 1910
Metal	Dog	Feb. 10, 1910 to Jan. 29, 1911
Metal	Boar	Jan. 30, 1911 to Feb. 17, 1912
Water	Rat	Feb. 18, 1912 to Feb. 5, 1913
Water	Ox	Feb. 6, 1913 to Jan. 25, 1914
Wood	Tiger	Jan. 26, 1914 to Feb. 13, 1915

Wood	Rabbit	Feb. 14, 1915 to Feb. 2, 1916
Fire	Dragon	Feb. 3, 1916 to Jan. 22, 1917
Fire	Snake	Jan. 23, 1917 to Feb. 10, 1918
Earth	Horse	Feb. 11, 1918 to Jan. 31, 1919
Earth	Sheep	Feb. 1, 1919 to Feb. 19, 1920
Metal	Monkey	Feb. 20, 1920 to Feb. 7, 1921
Metal	Rooster	Feb. 8, 1921 to Jan. 27, 1922
Water	Dog	Jan. 28, 1922 to Feb. 15, 1923
Water	Boar	Feb. 16, 1923 to Feb. 4, 1924
Wood	Rat	Feb. 5, 1924 to Jan. 24, 1925
Wood	Ox	Jan. 25, 1925 to Feb. 12, 1926
Fire	Tiger	Feb. 13, 1926 to Feb. 1, 1927
Fire	Rabbit	Feb. 2, 1927 to Jan. 22, 1928
Earth	Dragon	Jan. 23, 1928 to Feb. 9, 1929
Earth	Snake	Feb. 10, 1929 to Jan. 29, 1930
Metal	Horse	Jan. 30, 1930 to Feb. 16, 1931
Metal	Sheep	Feb. 17, 1931 to Feb. 5, 1932
Water	Monkey	Feb. 6, 1932 to Jan. 25, 1933
Water	Rooster	Jan. 26, 1933 to Feb. 13, 1934
Wood	Dog	Feb. 14, 1934 to Feb. 3, 1935
Wood	Boar	Feb. 4, 1935 to Jan. 23, 1936
Fire	Rat	Jan. 24, 1936 to Feb. 10, 1937
Fire	Ox	Feb. 11, 1937 to Jan. 30, 1938
Earth	Tiger	Jan. 31, 1938 to Feb. 18, 1939
Earth	Rabbit	Feb. 19, 1939 to Feb. 7, 1940
Metal	Dragon	Feb. 8, 1940 to Jan. 26, 1941
Metal	Snake	Jan. 27, 1941 to Feb. 14, 1942
Water	Horse	Feb. 15, 1942 to Feb. 4, 1943
Water	Sheep	Feb. 5, 1943 to Jan. 24, 1944
Wood	Monkey	Jan. 25, 1944 to Feb. 12, 1945

Wood	Rooster	Feb. 13, 1945 to Feb. 1, 1946
Fire	Dog	Feb. 2, 1946 to Jan. 21, 1947
Fire	Boar	Jan. 22, 1947 to Feb. 9, 1948
Earth	Rat	Feb. 10, 1948 to Jan. 28, 1949
Earth	Ox	Jan. 29, 1949 to Feb. 16, 1950
Metal	Tiger	Feb. 17, 1950 to Feb. 5, 1951
Metal	Rabbit	Feb. 6, 1951 to Jan. 26, 1952
Water	Dragon	Jan. 27, 1952 to Feb. 13, 1953
Water	Snake	Feb. 14, 1953 to Feb. 2, 1954
Wood	Horse	Feb. 3, 1954 to Jan. 23, 1955
Wood	Sheep	Jan. 24, 1955 to Feb. 11, 1956
Fire	Monkey	Feb. 12, 1956 to Jan. 30, 1957
Fire	Rooster	Jan. 31, 1957 to Feb. 17, 1958
Earth	Dog	Feb. 18, 1958 to Feb. 7, 1959
Earth	Boar	Feb. 8, 1959 to Jan. 27, 1960
Metal	Rat	Jan. 28, 1960 to Feb. 14, 1961
Metal	Ox	Feb. 15, 1961 to Feb. 4, 1962
Water	Tiger	Feb. 5, 1962 to Jan. 24, 1963
Water	Rabbit	Jan. 25, 1963 to Feb. 12, 1964
Wood	Dragon	Feb. 13, 1964 to Feb. 1, 1965
Wood	Snake	Feb. 2, 1965 to Jan. 20, 1966
Fire	Horse	Jan. 21, 1966 to Feb. 8, 1967
Fire	Sheep	Feb. 9, 1967 to Jan. 29, 1968
Earth	Monkey	Jan. 30, 1968 to Feb. 16, 1969
Earth	Rooster	Feb. 17, 1969 to Feb. 5, 1970
Metal	Dog	Feb. 6, 1970 to Jan. 26, 1971
Metal	Boar	Jan. 27, 1971 to Jan. 15, 1972
Water	Rat	Jan. 16, 1972 to Feb. 2, 1973
Water	Ox	Feb. 3, 1973 to Jan. 22, 1974
Wood	Tiger	Jan. 23, 1974 to Feb. 10, 1975

Wood	Rabbit	Feb. 11, 1975 to Jan. 30, 1976
Fire	Dragon	Jan. 31, 1976 to Feb. 17, 1977
Fire	Snake	Feb. 18, 1977 to Feb. 6, 1978
Earth	Horse	Feb. 7, 1978 to Jan. 27, 1979
Earth	Sheep	Jan. 28, 1979 to Feb. 15, 1980
Metal	Monkey	Feb. 16, 1980 to Feb. 4, 1981
Metal	Rooster	Feb. 5, 1981 to Jan. 24, 1982
Water	Dog	Jan. 25, 1982 to Feb. 12, 1983
Water	Boar	Feb. 13, 1983 to Feb. 1, 1984
Wood	Rat	Feb. 2, 1984 to Feb. 19, 1985
Wood	Ox	Feb. 20, 1985 to Feb. 8, 1986
Fire	Tiger	Feb. 9, 1986 to Jan. 28, 1987
Fire	Rabbit	Jan. 29, 1987 to Feb. 16, 1988
Earth	Dragon	Feb. 17, 1988 to Feb. 5, 1989
Earth	Snake	Feb. 6, 1989 to Jan. 26, 1990
Metal	Horse	Jan. 27, 1990 to Feb. 14, 1991
Metal	Sheep	Feb. 15, 1991 to Feb. 3, 1992
Water	Monkey	Feb. 4, 1992 to Jan. 22, 1993
Water	Rooster	Jan. 23, 1993 to Feb. 9, 1994
Wood	Dog	Feb. 10, 1994 to Jan. 30, 1995
Wood	Boar	Jan. 31, 1995 to Feb. 18, 1996
Fire	Rat	Feb. 19, 1996 to Feb. 6, 1997
Fire	Ox	Feb. 7, 1997 to Jan. 27, 1998
Earth	Tiger	Jan. 28, 1998 to Feb. 15, 1999
Earth	Rabbit	Feb. 16, 1999 to Feb. 4, 2000
Metal	Dragon	Feb. 5, 2000

Appendix 2

Personal Trigram for Year of Birth

Chien

Male: 1913, 1922, 1931, 1940, 1949, 1958, 1967, 1976, 1985, 1994

Female: 1919, 1928, 1937, 1946, 1955, 1964, 1973, 1982, 1991

Tui

Male: 1912, 1921, 1930, 1939, 1948, 1957, 1966, 1975, 1984, 1993

Female: 1911, 1920, 1929, 1938, 1947, 1956, 1965, 1974, 1983, 1992

Continued on page 124.

Personal Trigram for Year of Birth (continued).

Li

Male: 1910, 1919, 1928, 1937, 1946, 1955, 1964, 1973, 1982, 1991

Female: 1913, 1922, 1931, 1940, 1949, 1958, 1967, 1976, 1985, 1994

Chen

Male: 1916, 1925, 1934, 1943, 1952, 1961, 1970, 1979, 1988, 1997

Female: 1916, 1925, 1934, 1943, 1952, 1961, 1970, 1979, 1988, 1997

Sun

Male: 1915, 1924, 1933, 1942, 1951, 1960, 1969, 1978, 1987, 1996

Female: 1917, 1926, 1935, 1944, 1953, 1962, 1971, 1980, 1989, 1998

K'an

Male: 1918, 1927, 1936, 1945, 1954, 1963, 1972, 1981, 1990, 1999

Female: 1914, 1923, 1932, 1941, 1950, 1959, 1968, 1977, 1986, 1995

Ken

Male: 1911, 1920, 1929, 1938, 1947, 1956, 1965, 1974, 1983, 1992

Female: 1918, 1921, 1927, 1930, 1936, 1939, 1945, 1948, 1954, 1957, 1963, 1966, 1972, 1975, 1981, 1984, 1990, 1993, 1999

K'un

Male: 1914, 1917, 1923, 1926, 1932, 1935, 1941, 1944, 1950, 1953, 1959, 1962, 1968, 1971, 1977, 1980, 1986, 1989, 1995, 1998

Female: 1915, 1924, 1933, 1942, 1951, 1960, 1969, 1978, 1987, 1996

Notes

Chapter One

1. Quote by an anonymous author. Lyall Watson, *Earthworks* (Hodder and Stoughton Limited, London, 1986), 96.

Chapter Three

1. English language luo-pans can be obtained from The American Feng Shui Institute, 108 North Ynez Avenue, Ste. #202, Monterey Park, CA 91754.

Chapter Five

1. Lillian Too, *Applied Pa-Kua and Lo-Shu Feng Shui* (Malaysia: Konsep Books, 1993), 69.

Chapter Eleven

1. Richard Webster, *Dowsing for Beginners* (St. Paul: Llewellyn Publications, 1996), 110–112.

2. Richard Webster, *Feng Shui for Beginners* (St. Paul: Llewellyn Publications, 1997), 103.

Glossary

Ch'i — Ch'i is the universal energy or life force that is found in all living things. It is sometimes referred to as "the cosmic breath" or "the dragon's breath." In Taoism, the cosmos is regarded as being full of life, constantly creating and using ch'i energy. By gathering and cultivating ch'i energy, we can attract good fortune, longevity, and happiness.

Compass School — There are two main schools of feng shui. The Compass School uses the compass, the pa-kua, the eight trigrams of the I Ching, and Chinese astrology to make its findings. It is more technical and mathematical than the Form School. In practice, most feng shui practitioners use a combination of both schools when making assessments.

Cycle of Destruction — The five elements of Chinese astrology can be arranged in a variety of different ways. In the Cycle of Destruction, they are arranged in a cycle in which each element overpowers and dominates the element that follows it in the cycle. In the Cycle of Destruction, fire melts metal, metal destroys wood, wood drains from the earth, earth dams and blocks water, and water puts out fire.

Cycle of Production — The five elements of Chinese astrology can be arranged in a variety of different ways. In the Cycle of Production, they are arranged so that each element helps to create and support the element that follows it in the cycle. In the Cycle of Production, fire produces earth, earth produces metal, metal liquifies (which symbolically produces water), water nurtures and creates wood, and wood burns and creates fire.

East Four Houses — The pa-kua indicates eight directions which are divided into two groups: the West Four Houses and the East Four Houses. The East Four Houses contain the trigrams Li, which represents south; K'an, which represents north; Chen, which represents east; and Sun, which represents southeast. If your back door faces any of these directions, your apartment belongs to the East Four Houses group.

Feng Shui — Feng shui is the art of living in harmony with the earth. Feng shui literally means "wind and water." If we live in harmony with the winds and waters of the earth, we will lead lives of contentment and abundance.

Five Elements — The five elements of Chinese astrology are used extensively in feng shui. They are fire, earth, metal, water, and wood. Each element possesses a distinct type of energy, and the combination of the elements plays an important role in feng shui. In a Chinese astrological chart, you would find all, or most, of the elements in your makeup. The astrologer looks at the different weightings of each element to determine your personality. In feng shui, we mainly use the element that relates to our year of birth.

Form School — There are two main schools of feng shui. The Form School, by far the older school, looks at the geography of the landscape when making assessments. The shapes and orientations of hills, mountains, rivers, and streams are carefully evaluated to determine a site that is abundant in beneficial ch'i.

Fortuitous Corner — The Fortuitous Corner is the farthest corner that is visible when you stand at the front entrance to your apartment. This position is considered a fortunate one, and is the perfect place to have something that represents either your personal element or the element that precedes yours in the Cycle of Production.

Magic Square — A magic square consists of a series of numbers arranged inside a grid in such a way that all of the horizontal, vertical, and diagonal rows add up to equal the same total. The most famous magic square of all is the one that Wu of Hsia found in the markings on a tortoise that crawled out of the Yellow River some 5,000 years ago. This discovery led to the creation of feng shui, the I Ching, Chinese astrology, and Chinese numerology.

Pa-kua — The pa-kua is an eight-sided symbol that is used largely as a protective talisman. It usually contains a mirror or the yin-yang symbol in the center. Around this are arranged the eight trigrams of the I Ching. We can use the pa-kua to determine our auspicious and inauspicious directions and locations.

Remedies — Remedies or "cures" are used to modify or eliminate the harmful effects of shars. A pa-kua mirror, for example, can be used as a remedy to send a shar back where it came from. A simple hedge can serve the same purpose if it hides the shar from view.

Shars — Shars are straight lines of negative energy that carry the potential for bad luck and misfortune. They are frequently known as "poison arrows." A straight road or path heading directly to the main entrance of your apartment building would be considered a shar. If a neighboring apartment building were set at an angle to yours, the two walls pointing in your direction create an arrow that would also be considered a shar.

West Four Houses — The pa-kua indicates eight directions which are divided into two groups: the East Four Houses and the West Four Houses. The West Four

Houses are Chien, which represents northwest; K'un, which represents southwest; Ken, which represents northeast; and Tui, which represents west. If your back door faces any of these directions, your apartment belongs to the West Four Houses group.

Yin and Yang — Yin and yang represent the two opposites in Taoist philosophy. However, they are complementary rather than opposing in effect, and neither can exist without the other. Night and day provide a perfect example: without night, there could be no day. Other yin/yang pairs are tall and short, male and female, negative and positive, contraction and expansion. The concept originally came when the ancients looked at the two sides of a mountain. They called the northern, shady side yin, and the sunny, southern side yang. This dualistic view of the universe plays an important role in feng shui.

Bibliography

Chuen, Master Lam Kam. *Feng Shui Handbook*. London: Gaia Books Limited, and New York: Henry Holt and Company, 1996.

Heann-Tatt, Ong. *The Chinese Pakua*. Malaysia: Pelanduk Publications, 1991.

Kaptchuk, Ted. J. *The Web That Has No Weaver.* New York: Congdon and Weed, Inc., 1983.

de Kermadec, Jean-Michel Huon. *The Way to Chinese Astrology: The Four Pillars of Destiny*. Translated by N. Derek Poulsen. London: Unwin Paperbacks, 1983.

Kingston, Karen. *Creating Sacred Space with Feng Shui*. London: Judy Piatkus (Publishers) Limited, 1997.

Lin, Jami, ed. *Contemporary Earth Design: A Feng Shui Anthology*. Miami, FL: Earth Design, Inc., 1997.

Low, Albert. *Practical Feng Shui for the Home*. Malaysia: Pelanduk Publications, 1995.

Stevens, Keith. *Chinese Gods*. London: Collins and Brown Limited, 1997.

Too, Lillian. *Feng Shui*. Malaysia: Konsep Lagenda Sdn Bhd., 1993.

————. *Practical Applications of Feng Shui*. Malaysia: Konsep Lagenda Sdn Bhd., 1994.

Tsuei, Wei. *Roots of Chinese Culture and Medicine*. Malaysia: Pelanduk Publications, 1992.

Watson, Lyall. *Earthworks*. London: Hodder and Stoughton Limited, 1986.

Webster, Richard. *Feng Shui for Beginners*. St. Paul, MN: Llewellyn Publications, 1997.

————. *Dowsing for Beginners*. St. Paul, MN: Llewellyn Publications, 1996.

Wong, Eva. *Feng-Shui*. Boston, MA: Shambhala Publications, Inc., 1996.

Index

REACH FOR THE MOON

Llewellyn publishes hundreds of books on your favorite subjects! To get these exciting books, including the ones on the following pages, check your local bookstore or order them directly from Llewellyn.

Order by Phone
- Call toll-free within the U.S. and Canada, 1-800-THE MOON
- In Minnesota, call (651) 291-1970
- We accept VISA, MasterCard, and American Express

Order by Mail
- Send the full price of your order (MN residents add 7% sales tax) in U.S. funds, plus postage & handling to:
    Llewellyn Worldwide
    P.O. Box 64383, Dept. K794–3
    St. Paul, MN 55164–0383, U.S.A.

Postage & Handling
- **Standard** (U.S., Mexico, & Canada)

If your order is:

$20.00 or under, add $5.00

$20.01–$100.00, add $6.00

Over $100, shipping is free

(Continental U.S. orders ship UPS. AK, HI, PR, & P.O. Boxes ship USPS 1st class. Mex. & Can. ship PMB.)

- **Second Day Air** (Continental U.S. only): $10.00 for one book + $1.00 per each additional book
- **Express** (AK, HI, & PR only) [Not available for P.O. Box delivery. For street address delivery only.]: $15.00 for one book + $1.00 per each additional book
- **International Surface Mail:** Add $1.00 per item
- **International Airmail:** Books—Add the retail price of each item; Non-book items—Add $5.00 per item

Please allow 4–6 weeks for delivery on all orders.
Postage and handling rates subject to change.

Discounts
We offer a 20% discount to group leaders or agents. You must order a minimum of 5 copies of the same book to get our special quantity price.

Free Catalog
Get a free copy of our color catalog, *New Worlds of Mind and Spirit*. Subscribe for just $10.00 in the United States and Canada ($30.00 overseas, airmail). Many bookstores carry *New Worlds*—ask for it!

Visit our website at www.llewellyn.com for more information.

FENG SHUI FOR BEGINNERS
Successful Living by Design
Richard Webster

Not advancing fast enough in your career? Maybe your desk is located in a "negative position." Wish you had a more peaceful family life? Hang a mirror in your dining room and watch what happens. Is money flowing out of your life rather than into it? You may want to look to the construction of your staircase!

For thousands of years, the ancient art of feng shui has helped people harness universal forces and lead lives rich in good health, wealth and happiness. The basic techniques in *Feng Shui for Beginners* are very simple, and you can put them into place immediately in your home and work environments. Gain peace of mind, a quiet confidence, and turn adversity to your advantage with feng shui remedies.

1-56718-803-6
240 pp., 5 ¼ x 8, photos, diagrams, softcover   **$12.95**

To order, call 1-800-THE MOON
Prices subject to change without notice

FENG SHUI
FOR THE WORKPLACE
Richard Webster

All over the East, business people regularly consult feng shui practitioners because they know it gives them an extra edge for success. Citibank, Chase Asia, the Morgan Bank, Rothschilds, and even the *Wall Street Journal* are just a few examples of leading corporations who use feng shui.

Feng shui is the art of living in harmony with the earth. It's about increasing the flow of *ch'i* in your environment—the universal life force that is found in all living things. Chances are, if you're feeling stuck in your career, your ch'i is also stuck; getting it moving again will benefit you in all areas of your life. Whether you want to increase productivity in your factory, decrease employee turnover in your office, increase sales in your retail store, or bring more customers to your home consulting business, *Feng Shui for the Workplace* offers the tips and solutions for every business scenario. Individual employees can even use this book to decorate their work space for better job satisfaction.

1-56718-808-7
192 pp., 5 ¼ x 8, illus. $9.95

FENG SHUI FOR SUCCESS & HAPPINESS
Richard Webster

"If you want to be happy," a wise man once said, "be happy!" However, it is not always easy to remain happy when your environment is working against you. Your home should be a place where you can completely be yourself. You should be able to relax there and forget all the cares and problems of the outside world. Consequently, many of your happiest moments should be spent in your home.

The ancient Chinese noticed that different environments had a direct bearing on contentment and even luck. Later on, these factors would become known as feng shui, the art of living in harmony with the earth. Whether you live in a one-room apartment or a sprawling mansion, *Feng Shui for Success & Happiness* (part of Richard Webster's *Feng Shui* series), will show you how to activate the energy, or ch'i, in your home to improve your environment and to achieve happiness and abundance.

1-56718-815-X
168 pp., 5 ¼ x 8, illus. $9.95